Will China's Economy Collapse?

Ann Lee

———

Will China's Economy Collapse?

polity

First published in 2017 by Polity Press

Polity Press
65 Bridge Street
Cambridge CB2 1UR, UK

Polity Press
350 Main Street
Malden, MA 02148, USA

ISBN-13: 978-1-5095-2013-8
ISBN-13: 978-1-5095-2014-5 (pb)

A catalogue record for this book is available from the British Library.

Typeset in 11/15 Sabon
by Servis Filmsetting Ltd, Stockport, Cheshire
Printed and bound in United Kingdom by Clays Ltd, St Ives PLC

The publisher has used its best endeavours to ensure that the URLs for external websites referred to in this book are correct and active at the time of going to press. However, the publisher has no responsibility for the websites and can make no guarantee that a site will remain live or that the content is or will remain appropriate.

Every effort has been made to trace all copyright holders, but if any have been inadvertently overlooked the publisher will be pleased to include any necessary credits in any subsequent reprint or edition.

For further information on Polity, visit our website:
politybooks.com

Contents

Acknowledgments

I want to extend a warm thanks to Dr Louise Knight for approaching me to write this book. I have given speeches about this topic on a number of occasions, but putting it in writing has enabled me to flesh out my argument. I also want to express deep gratitude to Frank Arlinghaus, Alex Castaldo, and Dominieck Dutoo for their feedback on early drafts of my manuscript. A tremendous thank you goes to Javier Hernandez, who provided extensive legal assistance and generosity in numerous other ways. And my biggest thanks go to my parents and my brother John for their unending love and support for all that I do in life.

Preface

Will China's economy collapse? Many informed people have publicly stated that they believe it will. Books that have prognosticated this outcome declared this state of emergency over a decade ago. While China has not yet collapsed as of this writing, many hold on to the belief that such a calamity remains imminent. There are numerous logical and compelling reasons to support a scenario of collapse. Without doubt the growing uncertainties around the world have added to this fear. Moreover, as China is the largest trading nation in the world and second largest economy as of 2016, there is an underlying fear that, according to the popular saying, if it sneezes, the world will catch a cold. Events such as China's stock market crashes during the summer of 2015 and January 2016 in addition to the well-publicized existence of its ghost cities and its shadow banking industry have investors and politicians alike increasingly worried.

Although there is no specific definition of economic collapse, there is a general consensus that it is a situation in which there is a sudden occurrence of extreme negative conditions that then persist in the economy for a prolonged period. Various manifestations of an economic collapse could include any combination of the following conditions: an unusually high number of bankruptcies, high unemployment, breakdowns in civil society, increasing mortality rates, and widespread famine. History is littered with such scenarios.

While the reasons behind the collapses vary across continents and centuries, there appear to be some common themes and cycles. One common pattern is that when countries or empires undergo disruptive social change like growing liberalization, economies often experience high growth. This was the case both in the ancient world and in medieval times when growing social and economic liberalization paved the way for the Greek and Roman empires and the Spanish Empire, respectively. However, when these countries and empires overstretch themselves in military adventures, economic collapses often follow. In the case of the Roman Empire, once the army took control (ca. AD 276–401), they taxed the middle class out of existence to fund expensive wars so that all that remained was a slave underclass. Spain's ongoing wars also led to its collapse as a global power in the seventeenth century. In more recent examples, Great Britain's empire began with the nation's industrialization, which likewise coincided with growing social and economic liberalization during the eighteenth and nineteenth centuries. Similarly, the end of *Pax Britannica* coincided with involvement in two world wars. The Soviet Union also experienced rapid growth following the Communist takeover, which liberalized its society from generations of feudalism. However, its economy collapsed in the 1980s after engaging in a decades-long Cold War against the United States.

Whether China will undergo an economic collapse comparable to the examples above is something to explore. Like the aforementioned cases, it has experienced growing economic liberalization in the last few decades that has enabled it to attain its current superior economic status. However, many in the West now wonder whether China is on the brink of collapse since they believe its financial system, military program, and growth model are opaque and unsustainable. While it is impossible to cover all possible scenarios given the infinite number of variables that would need to be taken into account for a truly comprehensive analysis, in this book we will explore the most probable causes of economic crisis in China. Common arguments for an imminent collapse will be dissected and subsequently found to be grossly exaggerated. Years of working in the financial markets and countless discussions with policymakers and regulators have shown me time and again that reality does not necessarily line up with academic theory. But let's first begin by analyzing the vulnerable aspects of China's economy to discern whether they are indeed sufficiently weak to generate forces that could have catastrophic domestic and global consequences.

1

The Modern Chinese Economy: The Good, the Bad, and the Ugly

China's modern economy is an intricately complex web of state capitalism, laissez-faire capitalism, Keynesian economics, Austrian economics, Soviet-inspired planning, and good old-fashioned entrepreneurialism. Contradictions are a fact of life in the Chinese economy, and no simple definition or ideology can adequately describe everything that it encapsulates. One of the reasons for this complexity is that China is simply too large to manage uniformly. With 56 recognized ethnic groups practicing close to 300 living languages and spread over 3.7 million square miles among over 1.3 billion people, China gives rise to as many variations in economic activity as there are on the planet.

Despite such variability, China managed to modernize as one country with a speed that truly was unforeseen. For the past quarter-century, its miraculous growth has resulted in bringing the equivalent of the entire US population into the middle-income bracket. This remains the biggest economic news of our lifetime. China largely achieved this feat through a combination of exports and investments, which, as a percentage of gross domestic product (GDP), remain among the highest in the world. While other nations such as South Korea and Japan have also grown rapidly in past decades to achieve developed country status, the scale and duration of growth that China has achieved remain unparalleled. Some of the factors that distinguish China from other countries were the subject of my prior book, *What the US Can Learn from China*.[1] As noted there, China's leaders adopted a number of approaches that minimized problems and enhanced the probability of better outcomes for the nation as a whole.

However, there have been some developments in China that many find concerning. From strong capital outflows to volatile stock markets, a rising chorus of pundits such as David Shambaugh predict an economic crisis for the country. When China began developing, it was a small trading state and thus had tremendous room for growth by taking market share at the expense of other countries. Initially, it followed the same growth model adopted decades earlier by the four Asian Tigers of South Korea, Hong Kong, Taiwan, and Singapore. As they demonstrated, economic growth is primarily determined by (1) domestic economic competition, (2) infant industry protection, (3) state control of financial resources and international capital flows, (4) incentives that promote industrial production and exports, and (5) labor movement from rural to urban settings coupled with productivity increases. The principles driving growth haven't changed. Today, as the largest trading nation in the world, China is nonetheless constrained by the size of the world economy. It can no longer grow faster than the world economy through trade alone.

The problem of overcapacity emerged more severely in China since the world was unable to absorb its exports, resulting in a slowing of its export engine. This overcapacity led to even more severe price cuts and eventually massive layoffs of workers, who, during the 2008 financial crisis, were no longer needed in factories for everything from textiles to steel. For instance, China has the capacity to export two-thirds of the world's steel, but the world only needs half of China's steel production. Thus, in an attempt to forestall worker unrest, Chinese policymakers created a second engine of growth by inducing heavy investment domestically in the years immediately following the financial crisis of 2008 in order to rehire the unemployed workforce. China's second growth engine was characterized by infrastructure investments of all types, from sophisticated water treatment systems to rampant real estate investments that created entirely new cities out of the blue. Yet, even domestic infrastructure investments that were needed to offset the drop in exports have hit their limit for China. High-speed trains have now been constructed all over the country, and real estate expansion among third-tier cities lacks the residents and commercial activity to sustain it. A third engine of growth is now needed to keep China growing in order to lift the rest of its population out of poverty.

Developing a third engine of growth while the two former engines are slowing dramatically is challenging in itself, but the difficulty is compounded in China by its ballooning debt.

The problem with China's credit growth is that the country had already accumulated vast amounts of both public and private debt in order to fund its second leg of growth following the 2008 financial crisis. China's debt increase since 2009 has been faster than the debt buildup that occurred in the United States before the global financial crisis. Since China's GDP did not grow commensurately, its debt-to-GDP ratio has also shot up. The continued growth of its credit while its GDP growth continues its downward trajectory has caused many people to predict that the country is headed for an inevitable debt crisis that will bring about the collapse of its economy.

A Closer Look at China's Debt Situation

Throughout the modern world, the phenomenon of financial crisis usually results from a prolonged cyclical credit surge that leads to widespread and sustained deterioration in various financial and economic indicators. Hyman Minsky, an economist who observed these cycles, documented this pattern of financial fragility. The question is whether China's set of circumstances will follow this template.

While it is undeniable that there are signs that China's economy does not seem as robust as in years past, its broad economic health actually appears rather stable. Yes, its debt is sharply higher, but that alone cannot trigger a crisis. When one examines its other economic indicators, one sees a different story which doesn't fit the stereotypical picture of the prelude to an economic crisis. For one, China's GDP growth has continued to be among the highest in the world for over two decades while its inflation and unemployment levels remain consistently low. China also has largely maintained a current account surplus even at its more advanced stage. This surplus has shrunk considerably in recent years, but it still contributes to the country's enormous foreign exchange reserves. Despite sharp drops in 2015 and 2016, these reserves continue to be the highest in the world and can be used as an effective buffer against financial contagion. China also has modest fiscal deficits that give its government additional financial leeway for future action. The country's high savings rates at roughly 50% could also potentially drive growth. Most importantly, China has very low external debt, which is no more than 10% of its GDP.[2] By way of contrast, Japan's foreign debt is 60% of its GDP. With such low external debt, China would not be under threat from a foreign entity for repaying its debt under less than ideal conditions and thus avoid "the sudden stop" to its economy that other nations with high external debt have suffered.

China's banks are also financially healthy. They have a very low number of non-performing loans in their portfolios (around 2%),[3] are more transparent than the large US banks such as JP Morgan, and, despite the removal of the 75% cap on loan-to-deposit ratios, generally rely less on interbank lending to service their daily liquidity needs than do Western banks. Finally, unlike large US banks that count on large institutional clients with leveraged assets, Chinese banks rely mostly on the savings of the large population of households for their funding and thus are not likely to experience a crisis stemming from a single client, as was the case with the US banks during the Long-Term Capital crisis.

Bear in mind that historically most financial crises have stemmed from fiscal irresponsibility, financial exuberance, or some mixture of the two. China's debt problem, by contrast, originated when its government acted responsibly by creating an emergency stimulus package to neutralize the negative fallout from the global financial crisis in 2008, a move which explains why the country's debt level is an outlier among otherwise strong economic indicators. The stimulus package came via the state-owned banks, which were forced to lend because the government felt this was a more efficient way of increasing the money supply into the economy than through its fiscal budget. Most of the lending went to other state-owned enterprises (SOEs) and to local governments, since these entities had the capacity to employ large numbers of workers who had been laid off during the global financial crisis.

Although the government reduced bank lending by almost half when the crisis abated a year later, informal non-bank lending provided the fuel to keep the economic engine chugging. The bank stimulus and informal credit channels jointly created a surge of debt in China that had reached 250% of GDP,[4] an increase of over 60% over the next five-year period.[5] This figure, though higher than that in most developing countries, remains low compared to advanced economies. Japan's central government debt alone, for instance, is around 230% of GDP, according to the *CIA Factbook*, and its total debt has topped 600%.[6] The question of collapse is driven not so much by the quantity of debt outstanding as by its quality and relation to the economy, which could create potential vulnerabilities for a financial crisis.

Corporate Debt

The vast majority of China's debt increase came from corporate debt. As mentioned earlier, the bank lending from the stimulus package went largely to other SOEs. As it turned out, most of these SOEs were in the industrial manufacturing and mining sectors, which helped build the infrastructure throughout China during this period. Unfortunately, once China's massive infrastructure building had reached its limit, these SOEs were no longer productive. With these SOEs experiencing falling revenues and profits, these debts, which are still accumulating, could eventually reach crisis proportions if they are unable to be serviced.

While high corporate leverage is a worry, however, they are far from crisis levels and may never get there. *Business Insider* reported in October 2016 that China's non-financial corporate debt reached 169% of equity. By comparison, median debt-to-equity ratios of other East Asian countries before the Asian financial crisis were much higher. South Korea's ratio was 350% and Thailand's was 240% leading up the crisis.[7] More importantly, the trend of debt growth has been down. By August 2016, short-, medium-, and long-term corporate loans in China had all been contracting.[8] Finally, Chinese policymakers have been announcing measures to limit leverage like forbidding corporates to borrow if their debt load reaches 80% of its capital structure and introducing programs like debt-to-equity swaps, to reduce the likelihood that this issue will ever spiral out of control.

One approach that some people have suggested for dealing with China's corporate debt is to privatize the SOEs. The argument is that they have no incentives to scale back their operations to a profitable level if they know that they will be bailed out by the government. The belief is that privatizing the SOEs would reduce corporate debt and improve productivity and profitability. True, a change in ownership would probably manage to squeeze a few percentage points of cost savings in the short term. However, the downside to such an approach is structural unemployment, since many of these entities are located in parts of China where there is no other work available. The government could face a worse problem of worker unrest since the safety net of social security is not yet accessible to every Chinese citizen. Moreover, private Chinese firms are not necessarily better at managing assets. A number have run into trouble in recent years, such as the many companies involved in the solar panel manufacturing sector, because private Chinese entrepreneurs have had a tendency to hastily invest in similar manufacturing fields. They often compete with each other in a cut-throat way in a phenomenon referred to as "swarming." Rapid phases of expansion in certain manufacturing sectors were often followed by industrial overcapacity, which led to painful sectoral shakeouts involving mergers, bankruptcies, and restructurings. Finally, cost cutting can only go so far. The bigger issue is finding revenue growth. With the global economy growing more slowly than China's, it is unlikely that private ownership would make a huge difference gaining market share to grow the top line in a global political environment that is increasingly protectionist. Therefore, capacity utilization for many of these SOEs will continue to fall even in private hands. If the privatized SOEs go bankrupt, the government may still have to intervene and incur debt to support the unemployed workers, so privatization may hardly be a reasonable or realistic solution.

To get a sense of the magnitude of the problem, the industrial SOE companies in trouble represent roughly 10% of industrial assets.[9] If they default, the ripple effect would be contained since these sectors will not affect other sectors of the economy, such as retail or healthcare, in any meaningful manner. Even if the financial risks encompass private companies in this space, the financial shocks would likely be minimal as the government would probably bail out the entities viewed as strategic to the country's interest. Since the central government's official debt is less than 20% of GDP,[10] it has enormous room to maneuver when it comes to absorbing corporate debt on its balance sheet when necessary to keep the economy running smoothly.

Of course, defaults will happen and some have happened already. But that risk is already priced in the stocks and bonds of these companies, and therefore would not catch anyone off guard. Not only can risk be anticipated, but the negative impact will not disrupt the financial system since everyone will have made advance preparations to limit the fallout. Given that risk-mitigating measures will be in place, these corporate defaults will not trigger a financial crisis or collapse of any systemic financial institution since positive psychology and investor confidence have proven to withstand market reverses.

Local Government Financing Vehicles

When China was a true Communist country, the government collected a lot of its revenues from the profits of all its SOEs, which accounted for 100% of the businesses in the economy. However, when Deng Xiaoping began liberalizing China's planned economy to allow it to become more market-oriented, profits from the SOEs plunged from almost 50% of GDP prior to the introduction of the economic reforms in 1978 to less than half that amount by the mid-1990s.[11] This dramatic shortfall caused the government to overhaul its reorganization plans in the following decade.

Since that time, overall government revenue has stabilized, while China's economy has continued to transition into an increasingly market-based system. However, a new fiscal problem arose in that local governments who were responsible for generating most of the local economic development projects throughout the country also incurred most of the costs of these investments, which exceeded the amount they received in government revenue. A large part of their revenue came from selling real estate to developers and making money from the profits of land sales. Taxes from other sources have been small in comparison. While the central government made transfers to respond to the funding gaps, they were still not enough to close the difference between local government expenditures and income. As a result, most local government authorities have relied on credit to meet their cash needs.

Because local governments were forbidden to raise capital by issuing municipal bonds or run deficits, they created their own companies, called local government financing vehicles (LGFVs), to finance their operations. These LGFVs were used to undertake local government responsibilities such as building schools and other infrastructure. The

LGFVs were capitalized with cash or land through transfers by local governments and then used the assets to borrow from the banks and capital markets to complete their projects.

Like other companies, the LGFVs had to issue periodic financial disclosures when they borrowed from banks or issued bonds. However, when they borrowed from what were collectively known as "shadow banking" entities, monitoring the debt accumulation of LGFVs became much more difficult since there were fewer and less stringent regulations surrounding such activities. As a result, widespread angst over opaque debt levels prompted the Chinese government to conduct a comprehensive audit of local government debt. It found that shadow banking financing of LGFVs more than tripled between 2011 and 2013 to over $1T.[12] Though the 2013 audit counted a wider range of shadow banking activities that were missing from the earlier audit, the results confirmed nonetheless that shadow banking had become a material source of financing for LGFVs.

To address the transparency problem, the Chinese government mandated that, starting in 2016, local governments had to issue municipal bonds to meet their financing needs. Though it initially required all the shadow banking debt to be swapped out, it has since retracted that requirement. Even so, Moody's estimates that China's local government debt coupled with its central government debt will produce a combined public debt of about 43% of its GDP in 2017, which is low relative to that of many developed countries. Most countries in Europe and the United States have public debt levels of over 100% of GDP. Even developing economies like Brazil and India have higher public debt levels, at 66% and 69%, respectively.

In the worst case scenario, should the central government have to absorb all the bad debt from the SOEs and LGFVs, the government still has the resources to handle the losses. The combined value of the government's landholdings and the SOEs' net of debt is worth more than $10T, thus giving China more than enough to cover the total public debt of roughly $6T.[13] Theoretically, these assets can finance a bailout that can forestall any loss of investor confidence, though it will probably never reach that point. In truth, the risk is less about solvency and more about liquidity, since the government is not only solvent, but is also underleveraged by international standards. The fear is that LGFV debts have been financed with short-term debt while many of the projects they finance are long term in nature and won't generate cash for years. But the risk can actually be addressed by simply rolling over the debts so that LGFVs only pay interest payments, a solution commonly practiced everywhere in the world.

To further address the debt burden issue, the central government also allowed the LGFVs to issue stock in the stock market. The pumped-up stock market was in part an effort to sell the LGFVs' stock in order to reduce their credit exposure. As part of the reform effort, the central government also required local governments to improve their risk management systems and allowed them to retain more of the government revenue in order to better match their revenues with their expenditures. Finally, to discourage local government officials from making bad investment decisions, the central government changed the incentive systems for promotions so that the job performance of local government officials would no longer be based solely on GDP growth but on a broader set of measures for increasing productivity and improving environmental quality. With the central government being so attendant to all the issues surrounding LGFVs, even if a crisis were to materialize, it would likely be containable.

Shadow Banking

Perhaps the biggest fear concerning China's economic prospects is what many call its shadow banking system, because the country's recent credit growth has been largely funneled by it. It is called shadow banking because this sector has little or no regulation in China. Whereas China's state-owned banks are highly regulated and supported by the central government, its shadow banking system does not carry the same government guarantees because it often engages in activities that have minimal oversight by a government agency.

China's shadow banking, like shadow banking in almost all other countries, remains rather opaque and relatively fluid compared to the other financial institutions in its economy. And like its equivalents in other economies, shadow banking in China has also become an integral part of its financing system over the years. Shadow banking actually encompasses a wide range of financing activities because it is by definition anything that the authorities do not have tight regulatory control over. In China, shadow banking has taken on the form of everything from wealth management products and trust companies to internet financing companies offering crowdfunding and peer-to-peer lending services.

The Modern Chinese Economy

Shadow banking exists in China because there often is no other source of financing for the country's many private companies, which make up roughly half of the economy. The large state-owned banks which dominate the banking sector often have very strict mandates limiting the types of entities to which they are allowed to make loans. Usually the companies that qualify for loans from state-owned banks are other SOEs since the risk of bankruptcy from state-owned companies tends to be much lower than that from private companies. But since China had been steadily privatizing over the decades since Deng Xiaoping succeeded Chairman Mao, the number of private companies has far exceeded the number of SOEs. Collectively, financing needs of private companies also dwarfed their state-owned counterparts because the resources needed for startup capital as well as to supply working capital for skyrocketing growth rates once businesses have been established were significant compared to the assets on their balance sheets. In the beginning, smaller entities such as credit unions and loan sharks filled these financing needs by making loans at usury rates or providing the equivalent of venture capital from friends and family. But as the economy grew and financing became more sophisticated, all kinds of companies – including asset

18

management firms, insurance companies, and even the banks themselves – entered the business because the returns were much higher than in traditionally regulated finance.

Unsurprisingly, the ratio of the shadow banking system to China's GDP grew significantly over the years. From accounting for less than 30% of GDP in 2010, the ratio grew to roughly 78% by 2015, reaching almost 54 trillion yuan ($8.10T) or 27.6% of its banking assets, according to Moody's Investor Service. While the estimated percentage coming from shadow banking activities currently remains unknown, concern also centers on the sharply growing absolute number, because China's overall debt-to-GDP ratio has ballooned.

Many believe such accelerated credit growth accompanied by a slowing economy cannot be sustainable since such trends taken together would seem to indicate that capital is not being used wisely. As some commentators have noted, China is building bridges to nowhere with these loans. With no toll collection for these bridges, the loans to build the bridges won't be repaid, and thus defaults will be triggered that will ripple throughout the shadow banking system since the loans may be held in multiple institutions.

Historically, many rapid credit expansions have

indeed been followed by recessions or even depressions when large debt repayments have come due and gone unpaid. In Europe, there were multiple housing booms and busts, and the United States also had its fair share even before the financial crisis of 2008. What many fear will happen in China is that defaults on loans will rise, causing a domino effect not unlike what happened when Lehman Brothers went bankrupt in 2008. Since transparency from shadow banking industries remains rather challenged, no one quite knows where the trigger to a monumental bankruptcy might occur and whether too much leverage in the system will cause unforeseen collateral damage that may reach even beyond China's borders.

Clearly one of the major risks for shadow banking is credit risk. Credit risk is the risk that loans made to individuals or entities may never be repaid. The higher the credit risk, the higher the likelihood that the loan will default. In a country where rating agencies are embryonic and credit scores of individuals are largely incomplete, understanding credit risk among highly regulated entities already poses challenges. But when opaqueness is added to the mix because there are no clear underwriting standards among shadow banking entities, then the credit risk in the system certainly rises significantly.

Another major risk is liquidity risk. Liquidity risk is the risk that cash becomes unavailable in times of emergency or other related situations. Often, a liquidity risk happens when there is a run on a bank or other financial institution. When everyone demands their money back at the same time, there usually isn't enough to go around to satisfy all the obligations at once. In the case of China's shadow banking system, it is possible that if one shadow banking institution collapsed and dragged other institutions down along with it, the general public might suddenly panic over the prospect of losing their money and thus cause a liquidity crisis by demanding their money back when normally they wouldn't. This demand for money would cause institutions to sell off securities or other liquid assets to raise cash in order to pay back investors, depositors, or whoever demanded the cash. This selling pressure would at the same time cause all these assets to depreciate in value and thus raise less cash than was expected in normal times, further exacerbating the problem of liquidity.

The third major risk is maturity mismatch. Maturity mismatch means that the investment time-line doesn't match the payout timetable. As this applies to China's shadow banking, such a risk becomes problematic when sources of lending are invested in vehicles that have maturity dates that are incompatible with promises made to the lender of the capital. Often this happens when the broker believes that the mismatch can be rectified at a later date with a sale and/or purchase of another investment to replace the original mismatched investment. However, problems arise when the intermediary miscalculates and the mismatch is not rectified. When such promises are breached, this risk can morph into a liquidity risk and possibly a credit risk as well.

The final risk is the interconnectedness with the rest of the financial system. As the world saw with the Lehman collapse in September 2008, the downfall of one institution can cause a systemic domino effect across the globe. The risk some see for China is that the shadow banking system would overwhelm its formal banking system.

But despite the rapid increase of shadow banking and the opaqueness of some of the credit intermediaries, it does not pose a real threat to China's economy and growth. With millions of shadow banking accounts open and thousands of shadow banking entities engaging in countless transactions every day, it is inevitable that some defaults will occur. But the scale and risk profile of the entities involved will not likely lead to a systemic implosion even if the most vulnerable sectors are linked to the formal banking sector. One reason is that the three largest areas of shadow banking – bankers' acceptances, entrust loans, and wealth management products – altogether comprise less than 50% of China's GDP, which is well below the average of 128% of GDP for shadow banking assets in the Euro area at the end of 2014. And while China's total shadow banking assets, which include other smaller areas such as peer-to-peer loans, had risen to 78% of GDP by 2016,[14] risks in China remain in many ways exaggerated in comparison to the West since many of these risks are shouldered by the investors in shadow banking products and not the institutions themselves. Another way to compare China's riskiness is by looking at its share of the world's shadow banking assets. As of 2015, China's share was a mere 8% of the global total while the United States had the largest share at 40%, followed by the UK at 11%.[15] Finally, shadow banking entities in the West are also more leveraged and have products across multiple national borders, whereas China's shadow banking products remain within its borders. Thus the risk of global financial contagion is almost certainly going to originate from a Western firm and not from China.

The fact that China's shadow banking debt and

all its risks are domestic and not foreign in nature cannot be overstated. Not only will any financial problem originating from China not spread to other parts of the world, but China's financial problems won't even spread within its own borders. China's government has ultimate control over all the financial activities happening inside its formal banking sector as well as in its shadow banking because none of these risks involve another sovereign authority. This one fact alone gives China the flexibility and the ability to clean up any mess stemming from its own financial problems, whereas other countries that have more porous capital accounts will have greater difficulty in arresting similar crises arising from their shadow banking systems. China's financial regulators, like those in the Federal Reserve, can change rules and standards on the fly to address any developing financial issues. Just as the Fed was able in one single decision to turn Goldman Sachs and Morgan Stanley into banks that can access Fed funds or suddenly give itself the authority to guarantee all money market funds during the heat of the global financial crisis, China's authorities can also make equally sweeping changes to stop the spread of any panic that grips its own financial system. Finance, in the end, is a human construct and operates according to human design as opposed to following any strict immutable law of nature. And human design is only limited by one's imagination.

Still, others assert that second-order effects from a loss of confidence in China's ability to manage a prudent and reliable financial system could damage its economy enough to grind it to a halt. True, a crisis potentially could unfold so quickly that Chinese authorities will not be able to react fast enough to stop a systemic situation from unfolding. But for economic activity to collapse, credit channels would have to be broken to freeze economic activity. And, as discussed earlier, that scenario wouldn't materialize since the central government still has authority and direct control over its largest banks and indirect control over its shadow banking system. As long as the central government has no interest in seeing its economy collapse and can force its financial institutions to lend, credit channels will remain open and thus broader economic activity can continue regardless of what happens to the individual financial institutions.

Assuming the worst case scenario, China's economy still would fare reasonably if compared to the previous time when its authorities had to clean up its financial house. Back in the 1990s, China had non-performing loans (NPLs) that were estimated to be as high as 50% of all its bank loans outstanding because they were lending to badly managed SOEs. The authorities addressed this debt overhang by moving these loans off the banks' books and onto the balance sheets of asset management companies which were also created by the government specifically to manage the NPLs. These asset management companies eventually auctioned off these NPLs to whoever wanted to buy them while the government injected fresh capital into the banks. This deleveraging exercise, which is very similar to how the US government cleaned up the savings and loan crisis of the 1980s and 1990s as well as to the quantitative easing by the Federal Reserve following the 2008 financial crisis, enabled the banks to restart lending and help reignite growth in the economy.

Although China's shadow banking issues may be more complex to unravel than in the previous bailout, the problems are also less serious in magnitude. The reason for this is that China's economy is much stronger and much more diverse than it was during the previous crisis. Whereas public finances were a much larger percentage of the country's GDP back then, today they represent a much smaller share and thus would have less of a negative impact should China's public debt suddenly swell. China's authorities also have more experience and more monetary instruments at their disposal than during the previous period to manage another banking rescue. In fact, bailouts have already accrued to several bankruptcies financed by wealth management products whose impact has barely registered on the financial markets.

More specifically, China's options are no different than those used by the Federal Reserve or the European Central Bank for many previous debt crises. The Latin American crisis during the 1980s which resulted from overlending by US banks to Latin American countries threatened US banks with massive defaults. This debt crisis was headed off in the United States when the US banks were forced to restructure the loans so that the debts would be paid off over a longer period of time. Similarly, the European Central Bank together with the International Monetary Fund offered Greece a debt restructuring package that extended the debt repayments while writing off others. Thus, if China's shadow banking groups needed larger rescues from the Chinese government than the ones that have already taken place, the bad debts could be written off or restructured with extended timelines for debt service while ownership of various assets could be simultaneously transferred to more competent stewards.

The Modern Chinese Economy

China's Property Bubble

Since about 2005, China's property prices have surged steeply, growing more than fivefold in just over 10 years. High prices coupled with rapid housing construction have led many to believe that China's property bubble could burst and trigger an economic collapse. After all, many economies across the world have experienced housing bubbles that led to severe recessions or even depression. A property correction certainly can happen in China, but an implosion in the property sector that derails the entire economy is unlikely to materialize.

Why is this so? China's property bubble is unique in some respects because, unlike those elsewhere, the country's record rise in prices only coincided with the privatization of its housing market. One can argue that the price rise was only reflecting the inherent value of the land that had been denied a price signal under a Communist regime until a real property market developed. The steep rise in prices alone does not necessarily mean a bubble exists since the prices could merely mirror the true outstanding demand for the asset.

Indeed, China's record migrant movement from the west of the country to its coastal areas – the largest human migration in history – created an unprecedented demand for housing and urban development. While more than half of China's population has since relocated to the cities, another half a billion people still reside in the rural farmlands of China and have yet to urbanize. This fundamental driver will put a floor on property demand so that even if property prices cool off in the short term, there will be pent-up demand for the longer term.

Western commentary in programs such as *60 Minutes* asserts that China's ghost cities prove that this obvious oversupply will foreshadow an imminent property-led collapse. The 1 billion square meters of unoccupied space, though large, can easily be absorbed after only a few years of migration assuming that one person will occupy a modest 10 square meters of living space. In addition to migrant demand, the existing home-owning population have started to upgrade their living spaces, further driving demand. Although some ghost cities may become wasted, the vast majority have attracted occupancy once the Chinese government has provided economic incentives for companies to relocate to those places. Through any combination of free land and tax-free incentives, both domestic and foreign companies that have moved operations to the lower-tiered cities from the congested first-tier cities have been able to attract large numbers of people to occupy the existing housing stock.

Furthermore, unoccupied housing stock does not necessarily mean that property has defaulted or is at risk of default. Unlike the United States, China does not levy an annual property tax. The real estate tax is a one-time transaction tax at the time of purchase so there is no ongoing carrying cost to owning real estate. As a result, most Chinese would prefer to own real estate property unoccupied as an investment than to rent it out to tenants because it would appreciate faster without the wear and tear. Since China's stock market is also more volatile than real estate, most Chinese also have opted to store their wealth in real estate instead of the financial markets. Finally, China's closed capital account makes it difficult for most Chinese citizens to invest abroad, so these rules add to the tremendous appetite for real estate.

Though the Chinese property market saw small price corrections in 2012 and 2013, the prices immediately bounced back as soon as the government removed property ownership restrictions. The strong rebound was a sign that underlying strength in the property market remained robust, which usually doesn't happen in bubbles because of investor disillusionment. Even if the demand disappeared, the property market still would not collapse since China requires high downpayments on mortgages (e.g. 60%), while a large number of home buyers are all-cash buyers. Unlike the US subprime crisis, Chinese homeowners would have too much at stake to abandon their homes and leave the banks with an endless string of foreclosures. Since mortgages comprise the majority of debt for the average Chinese household, the low leverage in the household sector should rule it out as a trigger for a credit collapse.

The highly leveraged property developers could pose a bigger risk to the banks should property prices slide since defaulting developers would also have a domino effect on other industries that support construction, such as cement and steel. The knock-on effect could be somewhat mitigated, however, by the need for supporting infrastructure around property development so that these other engines of growth could blunt any economic losses caused by developers that go bankrupt. Moreover, property that has been seized by banks from defaulted property developers can be retrofitted into low-income housing, which remains in short supply in many of the largest cities in China where migrants have sought work. Debt write-offs from these projects could again be stretched over many years so that the losses would not impair the banks' ability to continue lending.

Construction will necessarily slow in the years to come as China's urbanization approaches an end and its population begins to contract as a result of its one-child policy, which was only ended in 2015. It would be perfectly normal to see GDP growth moderate by a half percentage point a year based on a housing slowdown since housing has been a large component of China's GDP growth over the past decade. However, a sudden collapse that would take down growth by a larger percentage based on existing fundamentals will be highly unlikely.

The credit growth fueled by housing has contributed to China's rising debt-to-GDP ratio, but this credit expansion again has been overblown since the growth in debt has also been accompanied by a widespread growth in real economic activity and a higher standard of living across the board. Unlike credit growth in the West, which has largely gone into financial engineering that has created far fewer jobs and greater inequality, China's credit growth has at least translated into real wealth across larger numbers of people, which is a far more sustainable economic situation. And with its debt ratio only a fraction of that in Western countries, it is hard to imagine the property bubble derailing China's economy in any significant way.

Yet the pessimists insist that the faster debt growth in relation to GDP could only portend growing inefficiencies that will eventually grind China's economy to a halt. While some of the debt may have been used inefficiently, the faster debt growth can also be explained by the even faster rising land prices. Fixed asset investment (FAI) measures investment that includes land values, while gross fixed capital formation (GFCF) measures only value-added investment that excludes land values and other financial assets. The fact that FAI growth outpaced GFCF growth in the years following the global financial crisis would indicate that the growth in credit to finance these real estate investments has directly mirrored the appreciating land values which are not counted in GDP growth. It would follow that once FAI stabilizes as the real estate market matures, credit would flow towards GFCF activitites instead, causing future debt-to-GDP growth to moderate or even decline. But in the interim, rather than a debt crisis that leads to collapse in China, the world will most likely witness only a soft landing in China's economic future.

2

Preparing for a Soft Landing

China's near-term vulnerabilities from a credit perspective, while numerous and seemingly dangerous on the surface, are in fact a bit exaggerated by most accounts. However, although danger is not imminent, it does not preclude a need for China's policymakers to ensure that the real economy is not also harmed by any sudden credit disruptions. So while credit from the stimulus was necessary to prevent an economic collapse in 2009, China now needs to correct the distortions that have manifested while also putting in place a third engine of growth.

In the short term, the Chinese government may have to bail out more LGFV companies and/or companies in the shadow banking sector should any of them be deemed too big to fail. Navigating China's economy in this period of transition will be fraught with challenges that may elicit the occasional headline in the media. No doubt Chinese policymakers will be tested should one of these pillars start to fall, and there will be plenty of winners and losers from both the public and private sectors should a full-scale cleanup take place. But since China has a strong balance sheet and a currently closed capital account, none of the scenarios arising from these problem areas will cause an outright collapse. Rather, a controlled "soft landing" will more likely materialize through aggressive use of fiscal and monetary policies should there be an absence of private capital and investment to take advantage of any dislocations.

Before diving into the policy options, one should note that a slowdown in China is inevitable and may be prolonged. Its transitions from an agrarian to an industrial manufacturing to a service economy have happened at breakneck speed for a country of any size, let alone the largest country in the world by population. So in comparison with past transitions, the current transition by China into an innovation economy that relies more heavily on research and high technology to power it into the twenty-first century may take much longer. This is because China will no longer simply play catch-up, but will have to start pushing against the unknown to make advances. It will also take longer because its leaders will now have the added challenge of managing not one, but two countries, since, economically and developmentally, the coastal areas will be distinctly first world in character while the western heartland of China will still lag behind as a third world nation.

Corporate bankruptcies, write-offs, NPLs, corporate restructurings, and consolidations could surge before leveling off to a more normal pace. To be sure, it will take some time to relocate laid-off workers and retrain them for new jobs when some of these businesses close. Many will not be reabsorbed and will rely on government assistance in the coming years as technological advances continue to replace humans. This will not be China-specific but a worldwide problem, though it does not necessarily presage a collapse.

Finally, China's shrinking labor force means that it can actually reduce its GDP growth rate quite substantially without it causing unemployment problems. The fact that wages have been increasing between 10 and 15% annually for over a decade means that China is experiencing a labor shortage. Like Japan, China can actually have decreasing growth rates while per capita incomes continue to rise. Thus, what some experts will call a "hard landing" for China will unlikely hurt the country as much as it will hurt all the other economies around the globe that depend on it for growth.

Consumption as Third Engine?

The Western consensus view for addressing China's slowdown is that it needs to shift to a more consumption-driven growth model and reduce its dependence on investment as its third engine of growth. Many people cite the extremely low share of consumption to GDP as indicative of repressed spending and believe that diverting the high share of infrastructure investment towards building stronger social safety nets will enhance consumer expenditure. There is some truth to that since many households often save for a rainy day when they cannot depend on social security or do not have access to universal healthcare.

However, a closer look at the numbers reveals that China's consumption growth has already been in double digits every year for more than a decade. Officially, China's consumption as a percentage of GDP was roughly 38% as of 2015, but double-digit sales growth rates have been recorded in many consumer sectors, ranging from movie ticket sales to fast-food outlets. Since retail sales have been growing at between 15 and 20% a year for decades while GDP numbers suggest lackluster growth in personal consumption, Chinese consumption figures might be drastically understated. In fact, Professor Wang Xiaolu of the China Reform Foundation reported in 2010 that unreported income was as high as 30% of China's GDP.[16] In other words, per capita disposable income should have been 90% higher than official data. His findings seemed to be corroborated by an admission from China's Bureau of Statistics that its household consumption figures were based on an incomplete survey that does not take into account cash transactions and provision of social services through barter and other non-cash means. Other researchers have also concluded that many other consumption statistics have been underestimated. For example, businesses often do not issue receipts to avoid paying the high sales tax, leading to underreporting of household purchases that could be as high as 15 percentage points of GDP.

There is also the question of whether consumption growth is the chicken or the egg. According to Austrian economics, growth leads to consumption, but not vice versa. Thus, if this is true, China's economy will not consume itself into more growth because the Chinese citizens with money are already consuming as much as they are rationally able to. Rather, the problem lies in expanding the number of people who have money to consume in order to push the aggregate consumption numbers higher. To achieve this end, only another leg of growth can lead to higher consumption numbers. Of course, non-wage sources of income such as rents and dividends can also fuel more consumption, but these forms of income are more typical of wealthy economies with large numbers of retirees who consume but no longer work. There is no empirical evidence that aging populations with higher consumption spending as a percentage of GDP have led to higher growth in those economies; the opposite appears to be true, as evidenced in places such as Japan and parts of Europe. So instead of seeing China's consumption as being deficient, it is likely that consumption patterns are approaching a peak as its millennial generation has a higher income and a greater propensity to consume. This phenomenon may last another five to ten years and then moderate in the decades to come as the population ages and the economic growth matches that of the global economy. Of course, the government can alter consumption demand on the margin by provisioning more services to households, but all in all, consumption growth probably won't explode higher from these levels. Consumption, therefore, should not be seen as the sole third engine for Chinese growth.

Where, then, can China find the third engine to save its economy from falling apart?

China has announced in its 13th Five-Year Plan (2016–20) that it will focus on several reforms that will unleash more efficiencies. To be sure, China's leaders are uncertain which of their economic initiatives will ultimately succeed, and thus they will have to try multiple avenues simultaneously, whether it be supporting more entrepreneurship and innovation or leading with more political initiatives. It is also unclear whether the government can successfully implement their proposals, but at least they understand what needs to be done and have telegraphed their intentions without ambiguity.

Alternative policy choices could include reforming China's tax policies. While taxes have been kept to a minimum in order to encourage more economic growth, growth could also be stimulated by raising taxes on the margin to discourage certain behaviors. For instance, implementing a recurring property tax could end the distortions of over-construction and enable local governments to raise the necessary revenue to operate without having to borrow to meet their needs. A higher income tax on the superwealthy could also help raise revenue to pay for clean technology implementation, which would be fitting since many of them were the beneficiaries of dirty manufacturing.

SOE Reform

One of the toughest reforms for the Chinese government to implement is to reform SOEs. Officials understand that the government needs to clear the distortions that come from government guarantees. With government guarantees, some SOEs don't have the incentives to operate more efficiently and lower leverage. But government officials walk a fine line between efficiency and social stability. Avoiding economic collapse is not just about maintaining economic efficiency, but also about ensuring the social fabric doesn't unravel too quickly. The calls to eliminate SOE participation in various commercial activities in order to clear the way for more productive private players to enter the market draw a false dichotomy. China can afford to let these less productive SOEs limp along while also opening up the space for more private companies in high-growth areas to come into the market. The money is not zero-sum. Government funding can flow to both simultaneously as long as the government lifts reserve requirements for the banks and instructs them to lend to the desired sectors. Finally, keeping some of these SOEs may serve strategic purposes too. Manufacturing plants can often be retrofitted to produce different types of products, and one never knows when more manufacturing will be needed again. One such example could be an unforeseen need for wartime production of military equipment. Thus, as long as there still exist good reasons for keeping the SOEs, their reform will likely be slow and measured and eliminating them will not serve as the panacea for what ails the Chinese economy.

Monetary Policies

In many ways, China's monetary policies are the most conservative in modern times. While the rest of the world has experimented in monetary stimulus with negative interest rates and other unconventional means, China has remained prudent in its monetary behavior. With high reserve rates and relatively high interest rates compared with the rest of the Western world, China has lots of room to create more accommodative credit should economic conditions worsen. Rate cuts, loosening of loan quotas, and lowered reserve rates could all cushion any economic shocks and keep China from collapsing.

More importantly, China's monetary policies are sometimes tailored to specific industries. Realizing that monetary policies can be a blunt instrument, its monetary authorities have experimented in one area: targeted easing. By specifically instructing its banks to only provide loans to certain industries, it can achieve a healthier spectrum of credit risk throughout its economy. Thus if one sector, such as real estate, were to overheat, the banks would shut off loans to that sector and redirect their loans to another sector that may not have had easy access to loans before. Spreading the credit risk in such a manner helps dampen speculative bubbles and enables China's economy to grow in a more balanced fashion so that no one industry dominates. A balanced economy will also ensure a wide range of skills and knowledge amongst the population, which will make it easier to adapt to changes in the global economy much more quickly.

In contrast, the United States only uses tax policies to target specific industries which are less effective since they require the actors to be in a position to take advantage of the tax policies in the first place. In other words, one must be in a position of wealth in order for the fiscal incentives to work. If one is too poor to pay taxes, those tax policies will have no impact on economic behavior. Such passive incentives will have a much more muted effect than a direct injection of capital that can potentially come from monetary policies. Unfortunately, when the Federal Reserve eases monetary policies, it doesn't target specific industries. Instead, the Fed's actions have the effect of only benefiting the banking industry since only the banks have access to Fed funds, but those same banks are not required to loan the funds to a third party. With the transmission process broken, all industries except the financial industry can potentially suffer from a lack of capital under this model.

However, while the Chinese have refined monetary policy to better suit their economic objectives, it doesn't mean that they won't also follow the lead of other Western practices. One of the key lessons that the Chinese have learned from the Federal Reserve and the European Central Bank is to keep monetary conditions loose in the midst of sluggish growth. Even if easy access to credit can further exacerbate certain bubbles, it will enable greater spending in the consumer sectors while also propping up the stock market so that more SOEs can eventually deleverage by converting their debt into equity. More capital also means that in theory more money can get into the hands of entrepreneurs. The danger is the risk of runaway inflation, but with inflation figures registering in the low single digits for several years now, this appears remote.

Financial Markets

Some observers have been critical of China's handling of its financial markets, complaining that the regulators were too heavy-handed when it came to stopping volatility. They have also accused Beijing of not liberalizing the financial markets fast enough by allowing more derivatives to trade and allowing foreign investment banks to create and sell those products. They claim that these restrictions have kept Chinese money from being allocated more efficiently, and that without more liberalized financial markets, distortions in China's economy will continue to hurt its growth prospects.

China's financial markets are certainly feeling growing pains as their regulators learn to navigate the operational issues and understand market psychology. They are not alone in their uncertainties, however. Markets all over the world have experienced periods of wild gyrations that have prompted government officials to intervene. The 2008 global financial crisis saw the biggest government interventions by the US Fed and the Securities and Exchange Commission to halt short selling and engage in other measures that were attempted to stop the free fall of financial assets across the board. Viewed in this context, Chinese market regulators did nothing out of the ordinary when they halted trading several times to keep their stock market from becoming too chaotic. In fact, it would have been more concerning if they hadn't done anything since it was clear that fear had gripped the markets and that a timeout was needed to inject some calmer reflection.

The recommendation that China needs to step up its financial market reforms is self-serving on the part of those who have Wall Street interests. Liberalizing markets is how Wall Street makes money, since it can create a derivative product to trade anything that is not set in stone. For instance, liberalizing interest rates and foreign exchange means that Wall Street can create interest rate swaps and currency swaps as additional sources of revenue. Having interest rates or currencies that fluctuate constantly doesn't provide more transparency to the end user. They actually introduce more work and cost into production since companies now must have additional measures to monitor for their business profitability. Businesses will also have the additional burden of paying Wall Street to purchase financial contracts to "protect" themselves against price movements that Wall Street itself can manipulate once these items are liberalized. This practice is in some ways a legalized version of extortion, analogous to the Mafia forcing businesses to buy "protection" from them to avoid being killed by them. Thus China's slow-moving "reform" in financial markets is actually a godsend to its economy since its millions of businesses could be easily driven to bankruptcy once Wall Street is allowed to distort price signals that are essential to doing business.

Misallocation of capital and labor in China will not be fixed through financial market reform, given the ease with which financial markets can be manipulated and abused by sophisticated financial players. Rather, misallocation issues will only be resolved by tackling much harder reforms in labor markets, anti-corruption, and fiscal policies designed to change the behavior in the real economy, not just in financial markets. Creating a more robust and sophisticated financial market could be a source of higher potential employment in the short term, but in the medium to long term, the financial markets would be a big source of unemployment. One only needs to look at how Wall Street has shed tens of thousands of jobs since 2008, replacing human bodies with computerized trades and other software. Many of these laid-off workers have not been able to find employment again since their skills don't translate well into other types of available jobs.

The best way forward in financial reform is for China to come up with an alternative to the US-led financial system in the event that the latter system implodes again, but worse than in 2008. This alternative system should probably look more like what Alexander Hamilton, one of the founding fathers of the United States, envisioned, in which financial players cannot hijack the real economy and dominate the financial markets as they do today. A viable alternative system is needed to keep economies functioning smoothly, especially if financial markets become so chaotic again that they threaten to damage the real economy once more. At a minimum, Chinese financial markets could have rules in place that would allow financial players to function only as agents, but never as principals. Institutional investors perhaps could be allowed only to invest passively like an index so that no single money manager would have the power to move markets to enrich his own pocketbook at the expense of millions of others. If China is successful in creating an alternative financial system, it is very possible that the financial market could act as an employment multiplier by efficiently channeling capital to more entrepreneurs, who could create ever more jobs in the economy, instead of the rigged system that benefits primarily speculators in today's financial markets. In any case, rewriting the rules is an opportunity of a lifetime, and China should be mindful not to squander it.

Closed Capital Account

China still has a relatively closed capital account despite its fast-growing investments abroad and significant foreign direct investments inside the country. That means that capital controls exist to monitor the flow of money both coming in to and going out of China. These controls were put in place to prevent "hot money" or speculative money from outside of China's borders from destabilizing its economy.

Speculative capital has had a long history of ruining economies that includes the Latin American crisis of the 1980s, the Asian crisis of 1997, the

Russian ruble crisis of 1998, and the currency war between George Soros and the Bank of England in 1992, to name just a few. The financial "market" is usually nothing more than a few speculators such as traders at large investment banks or hedge fund managers who control vast amounts of capital and use this to achieve political and/or financial aims. Ever since the 1944 Bretton Woods system ended in 1971 with the Nixon Shock, speculators have been able to once again use financial markets as a weapon to steal wealth from countries or punish countries whose policies they dislike. Today's speculators do so by moving money into countries by taking various speculative financial positions and moving the money out as soon as they have made a profit or see better opportunities elsewhere. A minor hiccup in a country's economy could turn into a mass exodus that results in a sudden standstill. In the case of foreign exchange, a bearish speculator can short sell, or bet the value of a currency will go down by selling heavily in order to pressure the currency to go in his favor. This currency movement may or may not be in the best interest of the sovereign in question, but the country has only three options. It can (1) defend the currency in the open market at the cost of using up foreign exchange reserves; (2) let it move in the direction of the speculator's bet; or (3) institute currency controls to keep the speculative positions from occurring in the first place.

China's leaders have opted to keep capital controls in place despite their announced goal to allow the renminbi to float freely in the market. This move served them well during the Asian crisis of 1997, the 2008 financial crisis, and the large outflow of capital from China's reserves during 2014 and 2015. By keeping the capital controls in place, the government has been able to keep China's foreign reserves from falling to dangerously low levels that would disrupt the orderly functioning of the domestic economy.

The closed capital account will also serve China well when it comes to dealing with the eurodollar short, which was one of the triggers that caused the economic collapse in Europe during the 2008 financial crisis. The term "eurodollar" came about because most dollar-denominated deposits held offshore were originally located in Europe following the Marshall Plan to rebuild continental Europe. However, today the term refers to any offshore dollar account anywhere in the world. Since these deposits are offshore, they are beyond the reach of the Federal Reserve and not subject to its requirements. As such, the Fed has no direct link to these private banks to inject liquidity should a crisis emerge involving a shortage of dollars in these private financial institutions.

Europe ran into trouble in 2008 with the eurodollar short because it does not have a closed capital account. European banks had borrowed Eurodollars from US money market funds and used them in their business, including the acquisition of US mortgage securities. Once panic set in during the global financial crisis, eurodollars were all heading for the exits at the same time, causing a collapse in the European banking network even though many of the banks were solvent. The collapse could be arrested only thanks to emergency swaps between the Fed and the European Central Bank, allowing the ECB to lend dollars to European banks that otherwise had no way to finance themselves.

The European banks have since retreated from the eurodollar system by shrinking their derivative books because they can no longer make money trading the eurodollar market. This retreat has further exacerbated the global dollar liquidity at various money center nodes throughout the global banking network. Since global trade is done using US dollars, dollars are needed throughout the world to execute these transactions and are held at these offshore money centers. But because they are offshore, these money centers depend on each other for their liquidity needs as opposed to the Federal Reserve. Thus, distress at any one money center node has the potential to cause a strong ripple effect across the entire global banking system. The phenomenon of a rising dollar in foreign exchange markets, for instance, is often nothing more than a temporary shortage of dollars at just one of these money center nodes caused by a sudden demand for dollars by one or more parties, which is not unusual given the funding issues related to exports and trade finance.

As in Europe prior to the 2008 financial crisis, there is a eurodollar short in China, meaning that there is a shortage of dollars relative to the known dollar-denominated deposits in China, but no one knows how extensive this short position is. An approximation for how large the eurodollar short is in China is to assume that it is roughly equivalent to what existed in Europe prior to the 2008 financial crisis. The Bank of International Settlements had estimated that the eurodollar funding shortage in 2008 for Europe was between \$1.5 and \$6.5T.

The eurodollars that have found their way into China have come through all different kinds of financial institutions, which include not only Hong Kong banks but also banks from Japan, the United States, and other foreign countries. Since there are so many players, it is difficult to pinpoint the source of liquidity for these deposits. Adding to the complexity is that much of the borrowing in China also comes from offshore entities like private banks in Hong Kong, which also have a large renminbi exposure in addition to the eurodollar exposure. The fear is that if one of these banks suffers from too many bad RMB loans on its books, the eurodollar depositors might decide to yank their dollars out and cause a Lehman-like collapse throughout China and beyond because the Federal Reserve can't inject liquidity into the offshore bank and neither will China's central bank come to the rescue since it is a private bank beyond the government's jurisdiction.

Currently, capital flight from China has already been in evidence even without a dramatic Lehman-like collapse. Falling foreign exchange reserves in China amounted to roughly $163B in the second half of 2014 and $500B in 2015.[17] However, after taking into account offsetting valuation changes and capital account surpluses, the actual capital outflows were likely as high as a trillion dollars. With such strong capital outflows amidst a slowing economy, China's currency, the renminbi, coincidentally has been on a steady slide. Then when China decided to defend its currency from short sellers like J. Kyle Bass of Hayman Capital, it spent another estimated $100B per month for several months to prop up the currency from further depreciation. The rapid depletion of China's foreign reserves to maintain stable foreign exchange levels caused markets to question whether it even had enough liquid foreign reserves to keep the country running smoothly. Certainly, a sustained war with speculators who wanted to drive down the value of the renminbi has proven that Beijing could burn through its cash incredibly quickly, leaving market participants even more bearish about China's economic prospects.

The main difference, however, is that China has an ongoing policy of instituting strict capital controls so that the ability to take eurodollars out of the country is kept from reaching crisis levels. If eurodollars cannot exit, then speculators cannot forcibly make a bank collapse by suddenly pulling all of their money out. Thus even if China was eurodollar short by a wide margin, it would not affect it in a crisis situation because the capital controls would keep the money from moving until a more orderly unwinding of positions could take place. This would happen regardless of whether it was a Hong Kong bank or a shadow banking institution. Once the institution is within China's borders, it must operate under China's sovereign rules.

The closed capital account in many ways is

analogous to turning China into an island. As with a Zika outbreak, when borders are porous, contagion is easy. But it is much harder when everyone has to be screened before disembarking from a boat and mosquitoes that carry the virus are faced with a large body of water that they can't fly across. Likewise, a worldwide financial contagion will cause much less damage in China if it keeps its capital controls erected so that daily limits are put in place and every account is inspected for its legitimacy in money movement. This policy has protective benefits were another financial crisis to occur.

Internationalization of the Renminbi

By following the well-traveled East Asian Development Model of aggregating surplus from exports of basic goods, China managed to acquire a hefty foreign exchange reserve that reached $4T in June 2014. Of course, it eventually realized that these dollar reserves were of limited value if the United States were to pursue monetary policies that perpetually devalued its currency. With nothing more than a few key strokes, the United States could wipe out China's hard-earned money. This vulnerability kept the Chinese policymakers up at night, and by 2009 they decided to address it by engaging in a massive effort to internationalize the renminbi so that one day they could avoid being held hostage to the US dollar.

By 2015, the renminbi had become the fifth most used currency for payments in the world[18] and ranked second in use for documentary credit.[19] Although still trailing the US dollar by miles, the Chinese currency's quick uptake within just a few short years was remarkable. By the fall of 2016, the International Monetary Fund officially included the Chinese RMB as an official reserve currency in the Special Drawing Rights (SDR), further advancing Beijing's desire to move away from its reliance on the dollar for trade.

What effect will a reserve RMB have on China's economic prospects? For one, having a reserve currency will give China much greater latitude to pursue specific economic policies. Because it can print the money at will and still have it be accepted beyond its own borders, its reserve currency status will eventually become an incredibly powerful instrument that can shape both its domestic economy and foreign policy in the same way that the Federal Reserve can print money to serve US needs without fear of blowback from other countries.

An example of how China can use its reserve status to deal with its internal problems is in the case of its own shadow banking system. Should a shadow bank within China go bankrupt and potentially cause a chain reaction, Beijing can deal with it in the same way the Federal Reserve handled the 2008 financial crisis. By printing money at will to buy up troubled assets, the Chinese Central Bank can throw a lifeline to financial institutions that would be affected as collateral damage should a Lehman-like collapse occur. Because all the shadow banking assets are denominated in RMB, the Chinese Central Bank has complete control over how it would intend to find a resolution to the problem. Even if all the shadow banks collapsed and were not officially protected by the government, the Chinese Central Bank would still come to the rescue if the collapse threatened the economy. The Chinese Central Bank would face minimal costs to print more money to clean up the mess. Even if this action were to create more debt, the Chinese know that domestic debt can always be managed. Debt in the sovereign sense can be unlimited as long as the debt remains within the control of the sovereign. The Chinese government would have the same power to absorb all the debt as quickly as it created it without the fear of international rebuke, and thus what appeared to be an insurmountable debt problem previously would suddenly disappear.

Debt is only a problem if you borrow in a currency other than your own. If the Chinese borrowed that same amount of debt in US dollars from US banks, then they would have fewer degrees of freedom because they wouldn't have the power to forgive the debt or wipe the slate clean. They would instead be at the mercy of US bankers, who would find every way to enforce their claims, as countries like Argentina have discovered. But China's debt, like Japan's, has largely been internal, and thus will never act as an existential threat to its economy. The RMB debt that China issues outside its border and is held at foreign central banks is backed by its reserves of foreign currency and can be redeemed at any time. If the RMB value goes down, the RMB debt can be redeemed by the foreigners. If the RMB value goes up, the foreigners would gladly keep the RMB. Foreign central bank holdings of RMB would not interfere with China's domestic handling of its own debt.

Another way the reserve status will aid in China's economic prospects is that it will encourage more countries to see the currency as an alternative to the US dollar over time for transacting in trade and investing. If more countries used the RMB instead of the dollar for trade settlement, then Chinese companies could save vast amounts of money in foreign exchange transaction costs of switching dollars back into RMB and vice versa. As China is the largest trader in the world, the sum amount that it could save every year from foreign exchange transactions alone would be in the billions of dollars, which could easily be used for more productive uses in its own economy.

If more countries used the RMB for investments, this would not only help grow China's fledgling asset management sector, but it would also create a whole new global banking system that would challenge the financial order dominated by the US Federal Reserve. Instead of accepting the rules that enable multinational banks such as Goldman Sachs to create new derivative products at will or allowing hedge funds to speculate in commodities, a system under the RMB regime could have a different set of rules in place that could be more Hamiltonian in nature. The Hamiltonian banking tradition favors nation building, and if there were to be a rival currency and rival system from China, this would represent nothing short of a new world economic order that would once again favor the production of assets, rather than the speculation in assets which exists under the Western-led order today.

Preparing for a Soft Landing

A reserve currency status is more or less merely a stamp of approval for China at the moment since many parts of the world, including Latin America and the United States, do not settle in RMB. The inertia preventing the creation of payment systems and the lack of Chinese bank branches in these countries hinder the use of the RMB even when Chinese cross-border trade does not involve the United States. Nonetheless, the vote of confidence can be used as a stepping stone and will give the world more reason to use it one day if the world's central banks hold RMB in their portfolios.

The fact that RMB will be held as a reserve currency in central banks means that China will always have enough reserves in the event of a global crisis to supply the needed currency to these banks. China also has enough reserves to handle all its trade obligations. But its reserve currency does not mean that it can handle all financial capital flows, nor should it. This is an important point that is often overlooked. The reason is that even if China has trillions of reserves, that amount of money is no match for unlimited dollars coming from Western banks. The financial capital landscape is not a level playing field, and in that game, China will lose every time against attacks from Western speculators who have access to unlimited funds.

So until the majority of the world's capital flows are conducted in RMB instead of US dollars, China will still need to keep capital controls in place despite the reserve status. The reason for this is because what is considered a "safe" asset is no longer based solely on fundamentals, as theory would have it. In reality, confidence in a currency can be easily manipulated by the media as well as by speculators, which the world has seen unfold with the Euro crisis. Therefore, even if China does all the right things to earn "confidence" from the public, anti-China speculators who have a political agenda or simply want to front run their trades can create conditions in the foreign exchange market to drain China of its foreign currency reserves. Foreign exchange is the domain of currency speculators today, and unless China has the equivalent of its own Goldman Sachs to counter the moves from Western speculators, it cannot afford to open up its capital account.

Fiscal Policies

China has fiscal policies that are probably more appropriately called growth policies, because the budgets are often tied to aspirational goals for the country. In the United States, budgets are allocated to different departments regardless of their output. By contrast, China's fiscal budgets are accompanied by measuring sticks to determine whether the budgeted money achieved the desired outcome, albeit with lots of inefficiencies. Five-year strategic plans figure into budgets, and while China has often been criticized as being a bad allocator of capital because the central government can overshadow the invisible hand of the market, it is hard to sustain such an argument when it has not suffered the extreme boom/bust cycles that have plagued market economies and has developed faster than any other country on record.

China's fiscal policies thus can help avert domestic economic disaster since they are designed to support strategic growth and modernize the country over all other considerations. Through its fiscal policies, China can still increase infrastructure and social spending to offset anemic exports, for instance. Infrastructure spending could include projects for more subways, railways, environmental cleanup, and alternative energy. Social spending could see an uptick in senior citizen homes, more parks and recreation areas, and more vocational training programs.

The problem in China is that the fiscal system is

intertwined with the financial system. Since local governments have created companies to borrow from the banking system to fund infrastructure investments, the government is therefore in more direct competition against the private sector. Serving both public and private interests from the same institutions makes it more difficult to separate which activities are purely for profit and which ones serve a more public service purpose.

To make fiscal policies more effective, then, China has now allowed local governments to issue bonds directly in the capital markets so that the separation of public and private capital can be cleaner. With fiscal budgets that will eventually be more transparent once the bank loans roll off the banks' balance sheets, the government can more easily track which fiscal policies have had the biggest impact in generating adequate demand to meet China's already overly productive supply.

China's fiscal spending can have the most immediate impact by increasing social spending such as welfare payments and other programs that put money directly into the hands of consumers. Compared to Western economies, China's social spending is about half of that in other middle-income countries and only just a third of that of the rich OECD countries according to the "China

2030" report by the World Bank. Bringing social spending levels higher would instantly increase consumer demand and ratchet GDP up a couple of percentage points. But doing so could run the risk of destroying the strong work ethic that has powered China for the last few decades. Nevertheless, a carefully crafted fiscal program aimed at providing more support for the elderly, better healthcare for the poor, more comprehensive child support for working mothers, and comprehensive support for handicapped people would inject greater consumer demand into the economy without creating perverse incentives to slack and rely on welfare.

Belt and Road Initiative/Asian Infrastructure Investment Bank (AIIB)

China's leaders hope that by helping other developing nations develop in the same manner as it has, the world will experience a renaissance in productivity and the billions who still live in poverty throughout Asia, Latin America, and Africa will also join the middle class. China is so confident of this vision that it announced it to the world with its Belt and Road (B&R) initiative and Asian Infrastructure Investment Bank (AIIB) in 2014. The idea behind both of these initiatives is that China will partner with other nations to build basic infrastructure that will connect billions of people to the modern world. Airports, roads, railways, power plants, water-related facilities, and many other basic infrastructures are lacking in many parts of the world. China can lend assistance in the form of low-interest loans, technical expertise, and even low-wage labor to these developing countries when engaging in building needed infrastructure.

The global infrastructure building initiatives were initially envisioned as the perfect way to help fill an obvious need in the world while absorbing the existing excess capacity in China's factories and avoiding their closure. Indeed, the announced plans for the B&R spanned the Eurasia continent, the entire Africa continent, and major parts of Latin America. The AIIB would focus on financing projects in Southeast Asia and signed up 57 nations to be prospective founding members from Asia, Europe, Africa, and the Middle East to reaffirm that commitment. The scope and ambition were breathtaking.

However, reality has been more sobering than theory because political opposition from the United States behind the scenes with foreign leaders has stalled much of the forward momentum. A number of countries had been pressured to reconsider any such plans with China, or at least negotiate for more favorable terms when it came to kick-starting the B&R. The United States also pressured Japan to become more aggressive with the Asian Development Bank (ADB) in approving loans to projects in Southeast Asia that would otherwise have been funded by the AIIB. Though it seemed obvious to all that the AIIB was meant to be complementary to the World Bank and the ADB by taking on projects that were deemed unprofitable by the Western-led banks, the ADB actually was asked to engage in financial engineering in order to meet US demands. Financial engineering moves such as reclassifying a pool of money so that more leverage could be used were necessary in order to change the risk parameters for the funds to adhere to the original mandate.

Nonetheless, China pressed forward even in the face of US political opposition. It signed up many European countries as founding members of the AIIB despite US pressure behind the scenes to dissuade them. The real test for the AIIB going forward is whether it can deliver the needed projects to the host countries without defaulting on its financial obligations. The countries that do not have infrastructure investment are generally cash poor, so generating revenue from these projects will take creativity. China in the past has accepted barter transactions to make its projects pay off in Africa, but with so many other founding nations, it will be more difficult to find consensus on which projects to pursue and how payment will be accepted. More interestingly, AIIB bonds will need to be raised in the capital markets, so if commodities are to be used in lieu of payment, commodity prices will play a big factor in whether these projects will be viable. The other challenge is whether the AIIB can exercise its standards flexibly when evaluating these projects. Projects will carry different sets of risks and rewards that probably don't neatly fit a checklist. The World Bank and the ADB have been accused of being too rigid in their guidelines, like meeting certain "human rights standards" or "capacity-building guidelines," and thus have turned away many badly needed projects that would have otherwise qualified. Given this backdrop, the AIIB will have an opportunity to deliver if these political requirements don't unnecessarily get in the way.

China has also started the infrastructure construction for its B&R across the Eurasian land mass, which would start in Xi'an in central China and snake through Central Asia before going through the Middle East and into Europe. By initially focusing most of its energy on B&R going through Central Asia, China has opted for the strategy facing the least resistance, since the United States has little strategic interest in that part of the world and virtually no presence. But for China, completing this leg of its vast initiative would bring immediate economic rewards. The region is rich in natural resources, and the population there could become immediately more productive and a new source of increasing exports for China over time. The project will also speed up transport of Chinese exports to Europe, which will put other countries like South Korea and Japan at a competitive disadvantage since they have to rely on the much slower sea lanes to transport their goods to that part of the world.

Politically, China would gain too. This project could generate enough goodwill and trade relations that the Muslims in the region, such as the Uighurs in Xinjiang, who have been contentious with China in the past, would be neutralized over time. China could also minimize any potential disruptions by diversifying away from Singapore's port through the development of an alternative port in Pakistan for its energy imports. Most importantly, these infrastructure projects buy China time before a new invention comparable to the Internet can provide the third engine of escalating growth. By promoting infrastructure investment in other countries, China is not only redeploying its existing equipment and people to reduce its overcapacity, it also has an opportunity to promote its services, its homegrown technologies, and other standards outside its borders that will have an influence that will outlast the projects themselves.

Green Development

Green development features heavily in the China 2025 Plan and the 13th Five-Year Plan. Investing in renewable energy, increasing energy efficiency, reducing pollution, and cleaning the environment are key areas where China hopes to innovate and drive new growth. Not only is greening the country a necessity, but by treating it as a profit center, China will not have to choose between prosperity and environmental responsibility. Breakthroughs in this field have the potential to change the world.

Already, China is the world leader in deploying green technology. Investing over twice as much as the United States in alternative energy, China alone has more windmills and solar farms than all the other countries combined. But it isn't stopping there. The Beijing–Tianjin–Hebei Coordinated

Development Plan is a highly ambitious plan to turn these cities into eco-industrial parks that rely solely on renewable resources to function. The blueprints seem to come from a sci-fi novel in their scope and novelty, but if they can be pulled off, such cities will create entirely new industries in green procurement.

Top on the list of priorities for these plans is to embark on a full-energy transition from a reliance on fossil fuels to nuclear energy, renewable energy, and hydropower. It will create co-generation systems that combine thermal with electrical power and allow for a proliferation of micro-energy systems that can utilize many new technologies to fill the gaps of a micro-grid that will be more robust than the existing electrical grids.

The key principle is full integration of water, energy, land use, food, and information systems so that each system informs the others to operate at top efficiency. The energy system will make full use of wind farms in agriculture, solar panels on rooftops, solar films to cover the vertical sides of buildings, and geothermal wells for maximum renewable energy use. The water system will include vegetated roofs for onsite storage of storm water; eco-boulevards for wastewater discharge; biowalls to provide shading and transpiration to reduce cooling demand and building air intake filtration; protected riparian wetlands to provide filtration, habitat, and drinking water sources; cisterns to capture storm-water runoffs; and microbial fuel-cell wastewater treatment to process organic waste and produce energy to meet its own energy needs. Maximum land-use systems will feature more subways; narrow streets to promote pedestrian traffic; dwelling units that will sit above parking lots to optimize real estate; underground parking vehicle-to-grid technology that allows for charging of electrical cars all along the grid; and strategic density of buildings to optimize proximity to transit lines. The information system will integrate all the other systems together under a central nervous system that will monitor, price, and optimize resource recovery. For instance, Baidu, China's leading search engine, has already teamed up with the United Nations Development Programme to help solve the problem of recycling electronics in China.

The implementation success will depend on how successful the linkages can be made between the fundamental needs of society and renewable energy: green buildings will have to be able to provide adequate shelter; green transportation must satisfy mobility needs; waste must be converted to fuel; food must be harvested sustainably; and the environment must produce clean air and water. All of these systems must be approached creatively with an eye for introducing recycling and reusable materials at every possible juncture.

These mandates backed by capital will open up entirely new innovation efforts to develop new building materials, new resource management careers, the incubation of new technologies, and a whole host of other unexplored territories that will usher in a tidal wave of new entrepreneurial companies with unorthodox and creative solutions that will encourage new paradigms for living. The effort will have all the ingredients that would produce a third engine of economic growth if adhered to without political interference because it would essentially recreate a whole new China built on twenty-first-century technological expertise. This reinvention of an entire country would be nothing short of revolutionary.

To be successful, China will have to ensure its management systems will be aligned. Leadership must be proactive, not reactive from the very top. It would have to place a premium on system science, system engineering, and system management rather than operate through silos, which is the *de facto* way the government usually functions. All work will be a fine balance between cooperation and competition to achieve the best possible outcomes, and human resource development will have to touch the very lowest levels of society in order for the entire population to work in tandem on such a massive undertaking and become a much more successful innovator.

The challenges will be numerous and obvious. Education on this new way of approaching growth will take all the effort of the state to communicate, especially since it will be interdisciplinary. Equity will not be assured when taking down entrenched interests, and the economy and the environment will not be guaranteed to reach the ideals hoped for. Finally, internationalization of China's vision will hit resistance wherever inertia and entrenched interests exist.

But nothing worthwhile is ever easy, and there is little empirical evidence that innovation will definitely lead to accelerated GDP growth. Innovation certainly leads to increased profits and wealth for the lucky few who can capitalize on it, as the billionaires coming out of Silicon Valley have done. But innovation doesn't necessarily translate into broader economic growth unless policies are in place to ensure that happens. China's policymakers know this all too well. By announcing these plans publicly, they have all but assured the public that they will not shy away from what it takes to make this third engine a reality for the many and not just the privileged few.

Poverty Alleviation

Less revolutionary in its goals, but equally compelling as a possible third engine, is Beijing's stated goal to alleviate poverty and improve people's livelihoods. In order to achieve this "moderate prosperity," which is roughly the equivalent of Ernst Engel's 40–50% coefficient, the government will need to bring the rest of its rural population into the middle class. Modernizing the interior of China will require more infrastructure projects and social spending to increase rural consumer demand, which will continue to drive GDP growth for the foreseeable future. Since it took three decades to lift 300 million people out of poverty, the average development rate is about 10 million people per year. With 500 million people still living in poverty,[20] it may take another 50 years for China to reach this goal. Setting aside innovation, just trying to manage basic upgrading of the existing infrastructure in the western part of the country will supply plenty of growth opportunity for China for years to come.

Healthcare

Healthcare reforms are also low-hanging fruit for Chinese policymakers intent on driving engines of growth. In the coming years, the demographic dividend of a large working-age labor force that drove China's initial prosperity will soon provide a different opportunity for the country as its population ages. Demand for medical services, pharmaceuticals, and senior care living will grow exponentially owing to its rapidly aging population. Changing lifestyles and pollution will be the other factors driving higher demand for healthcare services. With growing numbers of people getting chronic diseases from environmental contamination and adoption of Western living habits that have led to obesity and other ailments, healthcare services will explode from current levels. Providing adequate treatment for all those who will need it will require large increases in government spending that will easily add to GDP growth for decades to come. But this area is also ripe for private industry investment since new drugs, new medical devices, and new senior care solutions will pay off easily with such a large addressable and growing market. As long as China's policymakers are willing to open up competition, streamline regulatory approvals, and minimize administrative red tape, private companies both domestic and foreign will have once-in-a-lifetime opportunities for record profits selling into this market.

Worldwide Recruiting

The Chinese know that expertise cannot always be transferred through reading books alone. Much knowledge gets communicated through experience, demonstration, and instruction. That can only happen with the right personnel in the right organizations. With this in mind, China has been actively recruiting the best experts in the fields of science and technology throughout the world. The future of growth and power lies in technological advancement, and China knows that it has a long way to catch up to the advanced military systems of the United States. By sending talent scouts all over the world, China courts individuals with promises of large research budgets, competitive salaries, and higher status in order to build state-of-the-art research facilities in every field of study.

This policy is not just aimed at recruiting overseas Chinese; China has hired nationals from Germany, the United States, Italy, and many other countries to fill these plum positions.

Taken together, these policies will not only keep China from economic collapse in the foreseeable future, but will also underpin the foundation for continued economic robustness in multiple sectors in the coming years. By addressing its financial vulnerabilities directly while also cultivating other potential growth opportunities, China's policymakers are trying to avoid unnecessary risks to its economic prospects. Like steering the *Titanic*, they are navigating treacherous waters, but unlike the *Titanic* crew, they have not thrown caution to the wind with overconfidence.

3

Even Black Swans
Won't Kill

The cautious attitude the Chinese leaders have about running their country extends not only to economic policies but to other areas of governing as well. From a policy and technical standpoint, China's policymakers certainly have the toolkit and the flexibility to handle economic juggernauts like an overly saturated export market in the developed world. But they know that economic problems cannot be solved by economic solutions alone. Often, political and cultural forces can exert influence over economic outcomes, and unless these influences are recognized and handled appropriately, they can undermine an economy despite good economic policies.

President Xi Jinping and the leadership around him understand this issue almost to the point of paranoia. While the policy reforms and identified opportunities have been widely recognized and articulated in their various pronouncements, like the 13th Five-Year Plan, President Xi's administration has devoted almost more time to its anti-corruption campaign than to any economic initiative. In fact, China's economic slowdown in large part can also be attributed to this self-imposed crackdown because Party officials have lost their incentives to take action on economic growth opportunities when they fear being accused of being corrupt and arrested. Luxury goods items that once flew off the shelves because people were using them for bribes now languish in sales. Why would President Xi put so many resources into an effort that would chill the economy in such a way?

The biggest threats to China's economic future and prosperity, in the view of some Chinese leaders, are the unthinkable "black swan" events that no one believes will happen. Although such events may seem far removed from current reality, it is also true that no reigning emperor would ever predict that his own reign would be the last or that anyone in Europe at the turn of the twentieth century could ever have imagined that a continent as civilized and advanced as theirs would ever be utterly destroyed by two world wars.

One of these possible "threats" could be another

world war. As a number of commentators have suggested, China's rise has been seen as similar to Germany's rise about a hundred years ago. The parallels from a political and economic standpoint are uncanny. A rising Germany back then was seen as a threat by the existing powers of France, Russia, and Great Britain since it could outcompete them for resources in Africa and Asia. These allies collaborated to counter the Central European countries of Germany, Austria-Hungary, and the Ottoman Empire. Using propaganda and other tactics, they pushed Germany and Austria-Hungary into an alliance, and eventually triggered the events that led to the First World War, starting with the assassination of Archduke Franz Ferdinand in June 1914.

Similarly, a rising China is seen as an economic and political threat by many in the US establishment. As a result, the United States has strengthened its security agreements with its allies in Europe and the Asia Pacific in a manner similar to its Cold War policies.

Surely, there will be plenty of observers who will debate these observations and deny such parallels exist. That is to be expected, since all political views by definition are controversial, but it does not negate the fact that the perspective exists. So as long as the fear is there, President Xi will do everything within his power to ensure that the security of China will not threaten its right to economic prosperity. As a result, Western sympathizers and possible traitors have been purged from Party ranks. But to weed out people simply based on political allegiance would be difficult to swallow at this point in China's development. The easier way to ensure public support for such a purge would be to clean out the ranks based on corruption, since this has become so widespread and so egregious that failure to address the public's anger on the issue would leave the Party's legitimacy in question.

The Anti-Corruption Campaign

President Xi's crusade against corruption thus serves two goals. The first is that Party officials will be discouraged from "corrupt" activities in which they use public office for personal gain. This public crusade will satisfy the moral outrage of perceived inequity with the hope that punishment of behaviors like overly conspicuous consumption and blatant bribery will restore a sense of fairness.

However, eliminating corruption in this financial sense isn't the premier goal, since this is precisely what catapulted China's growth. Unlike other countries, where corruption has inhibited growth, corruption in China shaped its development. During the transition from a purely Communist state to one that slowly liberalized and privatized, the state controlled all the resources, even if it didn't have a monopoly on all the good ideas. Thus, private actors had no choice but to convince state actors to team up with them. Often in such negotiations, they would persuade state officials to go along with the idea by using bribery. But the bribery was seen as acceptable because private actors helped government officials meet their growth targets, which were necessary for promotions.

Since it is highly likely that the Chinese government will continue to control its resources and exercise power over certain strategic sectors, corruption, by this definition, will also likely persist, even if it won't be as pervasive or as blatant. Some of the anti-corruption reforms have been aimed to change incentive structures that foster corruption, like removing excessive regulations or giving one-time salary increases to reduce the compensation gap between public and private work. But despite discouraging corruption with these symbolic moves, the partnering of public and private interests in such a way promoted rather than hindered China's economic growth. The importance of the government's influence over the SOE banks, for instance, enabled China's private sector to recover rapidly shortly after the 2008 financial crisis, so the government will not relinquish its role in the banking system, even if some see certain actors abusing their power. Even diversifying ownership by offering the public shares in SOEs will not change the fact that the government will have disproportionate influence over these entities. So while the current efforts will probably curb some rent-seeking activities and establish a more efficient and fairer system, corruption will also continue as long as the state plays an important role in facilitating commercial activities. Thus, the anti-corruption campaign will serve as a powerful move in terms of public relations, but less so in terms of actual substance.

The second goal of the anti-corruption campaign is for President Xi to consolidate his power. Given the dangers of foreign subversion and other foreign policy challenges, such as an externally inspired coup, along the lines of the abortive attempt to unseat Turkey's President Erdoğan in July 2016, it would be logical for Xi to ensure that he has complete loyalty from the people serving and advising him on all consequential matters. He shouldn't have to second-guess the motivations of the other Party leaders or waste valuable energy, time, and/

or resources trying to uncover possible traitors who might be planning later security breaches. It would be far more efficient to carry out the anti-corruption campaign early in his tenure before too many important decisions have been made and too much has been put at risk.

The use of anti-corruption as the pretext for arresting those in powerful government positions gives political cover to Xi to purge people whom he doesn't trust and allows him to restructure the organizational chart to ensure his complete control and security. Indeed, many observers have accused Xi of using the corruption campaign merely as a way to eliminate political opponents, since all government officials are probably guilty of some corruption under the official definition outlined earlier.

For its part, the leadership believes that its internal liberal critics have been unduly influenced by Western spies, who have tried to brainwash them. The leadership sees Western NGOs as outposts that spy and do missionary work on behalf of the United States. The Chinese academics and the media who have fallen for the charms of the West do not see themselves as being used as pawns, and certainly do not view the United States as an adversary. Since their perspectives on the Western agenda differ from those of the leadership, it is no surprise that these Chinese will criticize Xi's moves as being authoritarian and will sympathize with the US. But the more they condemn Xi's moves, the more he will be convinced he is right. His campaign shows no signs of letting up, riding as it does on the belief that China is entering uncharted economic and political waters where it is precisely trust and judgment that matter most, since laws, regulations, rules, and economic formulas will be insufficient to handle a "black swan" event.

Resilience

Given the numerous challenges already facing China, it is no small wonder that its economy has not already collapsed. Curiously enough, however, every time China seemingly stumbles and prognosticators declare that its doom is imminent, it somehow finds a way to recover and settle on a new equilibrium. What accounts for China's economic resilience, despite Xi's never-ending corruption campaign, above and beyond what could be explained by good economic policies?

This resilience can be attributed to several factors. First, owing to its sheer size and density, China's population has become extremely adept at competition. Growing up fighting for resources their entire lives, the Chinese epitomize the theory of survival of the fittest. A kind of mental toughness is inculcated when nothing comes easy. Since "necessity is the mother of invention," the Chinese have had to rely on their creativity and ingenuity to stay alive. It is therefore no surprise that when they meet with adversity, they learn to adapt quickly because managing change has been a long-established tradition.

Second, the Chinese rely less on the rule of law than do their Western counterparts. Without outdated and stifling regulation to block entrepreneurial ingenuity, the Chinese people have more freedom to create and start new businesses and industries. A rule of thumb in China is that if there isn't a law or regulation that explicitly forbids a certain activity, it is then safe to proceed. Even from a practical standpoint, the number of Chinese lawyers per capita is roughly 10 times fewer than the number in the United States. As a result, far fewer lawyers are devoted to corporate law and, by extension, even fewer judges are available to hear corporate cases. With so few lawyers and courts to service the needs of their business community, the Chinese mostly rely on old-fashioned relationship building, or "*guanxi*," to conduct their domestic business affairs, as opposed to the "non-compete agreements" and other legal devices that are increasingly used in the United States to essentially protect businesses from change at the expense of employee rights and opportunities. Local business, done the traditional way by means of a handshake, can save tremendous amounts of time, money, and energy. Since business conditions are often fluid and unpredictable, the ability to maneuver without the constraints of a business contract enables business partners to renegotiate terms and expectations more freely to match more realistic outcomes. This ability of Chinese firms to "change on the fly" becomes a real competitive advantage. Their ability to go up the learning curve quickly on their home turf has enabled them to become formidable competitors once they are strong enough to compete in global commerce. Western firms, by contrast, often have to navigate through mind-numbing regulatory hurdles and pay legal fees that border on extortion when operating in their home countries, stifling the ability of most small and medium-sized businesses to take off.

Moreover, when irreconcilable differences do arise between Chinese companies, most of them simply part ways rather than wait for their day in court. Without the need to put things on hold for a legal decision that can take years to resolve, the Chinese have the freedom to start new business ventures that can easily make up for any previous losses they have suffered from a past deal gone bad.

Third, Confucian culture, which emphasizes humility and the primacy of education, enables large portions of the Chinese population to combine their already competitive inclinations with hardcore knowledge to excel in whatever fields they apply themselves to. Because of this voracious hunger to learn and apply new concepts to the tasks at hand, the Chinese were able to scale the technological learning curve at a historically unprecedented rate. In only one generation, China went from a complete backwater society that was poorer than most African countries to one where advanced research in the sciences rivals that conducted in developed nations such as Germany.

While it is true that the Chinese have largely copied Western technology in recent years, this should not overshadow the deep technological understanding that enables them to reverse-engineer, without which even the most explicit blueprints would be worthless. The fact that in just three decades of liberalization they have been able to build high-speed trains, electric power generators, and silent submarines shows how far they have come.

This foundation or backdrop that explains Chinese resiliency is just one piece of the puzzle. The other half has a lot to do with the leadership of the Chinese government in addressing its challenges. As is the case more often than not, the success of any enterprise, whether it is a family, a business, an army, or a nation, is determined largely by the leader of the organization, because the leader exercises an inordinate amount of influence over the followers. In China's case, it has been very fortunate in selecting from among its population some highly capable leaders and policymakers to run its various governmental organs through its meritocratic system. Even though there have been failures, the overall leadership has been on the whole above average in quality. There is no guarantee that China will be able to find and staff the best people in the future. Obviously some question whether China will be hurt by the way President Xi has favored the "Princelings" over the "Youth League" faction within the Party leadership. So far, however, they have succeeded in proactively guiding China's economy with policies that have kept it out of severe economic trouble.

But collapses do happen when they are least expected. Debt problems, productivity issues, and corruption have all been identified and thus have been managed. But what about the less obvious scenarios? Let's explore a few of these potential triggers.

Shrinking Labor Force

Beyond the growing financial headaches that face China as it manages its transition away from export- and infrastructure-led growth, it has the unenviable problem of a shrinking labor force that will make Japan's demographic time bomb look like a garden party. China's demographics currently look like Japan's demographics back in 1980 when the ratio of workers to retirees was roughly 6 to 1. However, after years of instituting the one-child policy and with the growing number of women in the workforce, the low Chinese birth rates will yield a dependency ratio that will head towards 2 to 1 10 years faster than happened in Japan. However, in Japan's case, the country was already rich by the time this demographic shift happened. China still will have more than half of its population living in poverty when the labor force begins its decline in 2017. Even after reversing its one-child policy, the demographic trend has not shown any signs of reversing course. Thus many claim that "China will grow old before it will grow rich," and it is assumed that it will be a near impossible feat to grow rich with an aging population since retirees will be drawing resources from the state, not contributing to its coffers.

The assumption is that aging populations tend to be more rigid in their ways, valuing stability, not constant innovation. And the consumption levels of older people will likely be less than younger people since they are not typically expanding their purchases when they are not starting new families or new careers. In short, China's aging population could be a major drag on its GDP both because of its lower consumption growth and because it is unlikely to contribute to other growth drivers.

Japan's lost decades of deflation seem to portend what awaits China, especially since the former also experienced the triple threat of growing debt, asset bubbles, and unfavorable demographics in the 1990s. Once Japan's asset bubble burst, the value of the country's assets fell by 75% within three years. The dramatic decline in its stock market was matched by the massive fall in real estate values and in the number of full-time employees. Despite Prime Minister Abe's attempts at unconventional monetary and fiscal policies such as negative interest rates, Japan's economy has never revived. Not only has the economy failed to recover, it has only worsened since Abe took office in 2012, marked by growing hopelessness among its growing ranks of unemployed youth. While many point to the fact that Abe never quite achieved his third arrow of structural reform to reinvigorate Japan's economy, the fact remains that structural reforms are extremely difficult to implement. The impediments that block structural reforms in China could easily mirror those of Japan, since every country has entrenched interests who vigorously resist changes, especially if the changes do not favor the aging.

China's hope is that it can remain more open to immigration than Japan and retain a strong, well-informed, and well-intentioned leadership that will not be stymied by the same political obstructions which haunt the fortunes of most other countries. If China can maintain the same quality of leadership and power to implement necessary changes, then economic stagnation doesn't have to be a foregone conclusion. A potential role model is Hong Kong, since it has adopted a number of policies that have kept it economically robust despite an aging population. One policy example it has benefited from is to allow its senior citizens to remain useful in society by employing them in childcare and in care for the handicapped. Instead of just collecting social security payments, Hong Kong's elderly can help working mothers look after their pre-school children for a fraction of the cost of private nursery schools. Hong Kong's elderly also provide social work assistance to handicapped children, where hiring social workers can be a challenge. These are win-win policies in which senior citizens feel useful in society while being paid social security, and the next generations get to benefit from their kindness and wisdom.

Geopolitical Tensions with the United States

Unlike countries such as Japan, South Korea, or Germany, which were able to develop into modern, wealthy economies after World War II under the security umbrella of the United States, China does not enjoy the same luxury of doing so. In fact, since the time the Communists came to power in 1949, the United States has viewed China as an enemy. Although the relationship between the two countries warmed during President Nixon's historic visit to meet with Chairman Mao in February 1972, the political change was only for the purposes of defeating the Soviet Union as opposed to a genuine desire to alter the relationship from foe to friend. Subsequent to the disintegration of the Soviet Union, the number of surveillance flights by US Air Force in proximity to China's airspace has increased dramatically. These actions raise the question: what are America's interests in Asia, and how do its chosen allies reflect them?

Despite the animosity between the two countries, the United States could not resist the initial lure of China's abundant low-cost labor, which fueled American corporate growth in the 1970s and 1980s. Then, with the benefit of the Internet and other outsourcing capabilities, US corporations wanted to take advantage of China's low-cost manufacturing, which was even cheaper and more efficient than operations in much closer Mexico. Not only did China offer US corporations access to cheap labor, but it also did not have stringent and costly environmental standards, making it easier for them to make increasing investments there. Even after China's labor force became too expensive for manufacturing, its growing middle class captured the imagination of US corporate interests. With so much economic promise coming from China, US corporates such as Apple, Walmart, and General Electric lobbied Washington hard to keep relations with China cordial.

This lobbying effort by large US corporations

on behalf of China started dwindling, however, as President Xi Jinping took office. Xi quickly consolidated his power within the Communist Party and proceeded to fulfill his mandate to clean up the environment, root out corruption, and restore Chinese "historical greatness" in a bid to revive the legitimacy of the Party in the minds of the Chinese population. These domestic goals translated into less than favorable business conditions for many Western companies, which had grown used to the way Chinese did business prior to Xi's ascent to power. For example, Xi announced the elimination of certain tax breaks given to foreign companies to attract foreign direct investment, thus raising the cost of conducting Chinese business for many US corporations. And as a consequence of his anti-corruption campaign, sales of Western luxury goods fell precipitously as many of the purchases had been used for bribery. While these measures were widely welcomed by the Chinese people, Western firms' profits suffered as a result. Unsurprisingly, their support for China in Washington soured along with their slumping profit opportunities. The vacuum of support created an opening for anti-China groups to advance their agenda unhindered, escalating geopolitical tensions between the two countries, especially after the Obama Administration in 2012 announced its strategy of a "Pivot to East Asia," a system of alliances widely perceived as a means to contain China.

Although most economists don't factor such political considerations into their analyses of economies, the reality is that politics is inextricably tied to economics. Both are studies of human behavior, and every economic policy has a political motivation behind it that will yield a political winner and loser. Therefore, heightened political tensions with the United States will come at an economic cost to China that will reveal itself in many forms, ranging from an increase in lawsuits in the World Trade Organization and an expansion of more protectionist trade policies to actions that are more ominous, such as a new arms race, challenges to the One China policy, clashes in the South China Sea, and a potential collapse of North Korea. These political obstacles will have a material effect on China's development efforts because it will take more of its resources and more time to reach its desired economic goals.

One scenario is that these geopolitical constraints on China by the United States could become so onerous that it would have no option but to redirect its resources to meet these geopolitical challenges and thus collapse because its domestic economy is not strong enough to continue without government support. Such a scenario brings to mind the collapse of the USSR, in which the Soviet government had to funnel the vast majority of its resources to support an arms race against the United States at the expense of economic development. Once the Soviet Union could no longer sustain its military buildup, the domestic economy collapsed because there were not enough government resources to develop and support it. Since China is coming from an even weaker military position than the former Soviet Union, an arms race against the United States could weaken its economy considerably by extracting valuable resources from other key industries that need government support, such as social security, healthcare, and clean technology.

Indeed, China's increase in military spending as well as its growing military presence in the South China Sea and East China Sea, particularly after President Xi Jinping took office, has been closely watched in the West. China's military expenditure had been growing in double-digit percentages in the last few years in response to perceived US provocations such as the proposed installation of the Terminal High Altitude Area Defense (THAAD) deployment in South Korea, so it has certainly crossed a few minds that if it overextends itself in this area by engaging in an arms race just when its economy is slowing, this could bring about a collapse. However, China's total military spending as a percentage of its GDP has remained stable at roughly 2%, which is at least a whole percentage point lower than that of the United States.

Although China's military spending has increased in absolute terms owing to increased tensions in the Asia Pacific since 2013, it has no interest in direct military conflict. In fact, it announced that the pace of military spending growth would slow in 2016 despite the fact that the United States has stepped up military sales to its allies in the Asia Pacific region. Like the Central European powers during World War I, China cannot afford to fight a two-front war and thus will most likely back away from any meaningful military confrontation that would involve US allies. China's military stance has always been defensive in nature, not offensive, since it knows it cannot overcome US military strength even if it uses asymmetrical warfare. The United States is simply too powerful. With about a thousand military bases across the world, tens of thousands of experienced combat troops, and security treaties with dozens of countries, the United States can easily outmaneuver China. In contrast, China only has one military base outside of its borders, in Djibouti. It will take a long time for China to catch up to the United States militarily, especially since China's first priority is to strengthen its domestic economy and lift the other 500 million Chinese people out of poverty. Given this set of circumstances, China will not likely engage in any military conflict, even if provoked, so military overstretch will hardly be a reason for its collapse.

Even if a full-fledged arms race didn't develop, China could still face severe tests of its economic resilience based on other antagonistic tactics by the United States. The Trans Pacific Partnership (TPP) as well as the Transatlantic Trade and Investment Partnership (TPIP) are both trade agreements led by the United States that have a security overlay that is designed to disadvantage China from trade with countries around the world through exclusion. Although the Trump Administration has announced its intention to negotiate better trade deals, the potential ratification of ones similar to these two could put China in an equally disadvantaged trade position since it would not be party to the lowered trade barriers between the member states that make up over 60% of global trade. Should a full-blown trade war with the United States erupt, it could create an even larger setback since almost half of China's trade surplus comes from the US. Almost all industry sectors would lose in such a scenario except for possibly the US defense industry under heightened tensions between these two countries. Without an ability to generate employment for all the displaced workers who depend on global trade, China could face the same unmanageable labor unrest that an arms race would generate that eventually leads to economic collapse through internal coups and civil war.

Indeed, the number of protests and labor strikes has been on the rise in China. According to the *China Labor Bulletin*, over 2,700 strikes and protests were recorded in China in 2015, which was more than twice the number from the year before. Millions have been striking due to unpaid wages from companies hard hit by the slowing economy. The economy, however, did not have to slow significantly – only 0.2% – to generate so much civil unrest. One can only imagine what would happen to its domestic stability if the downturn was even sharper.

As a way to counter the dangers of mass uprisings, the Chinese government has actively monitored social media and blogging sites to censor any online messages that call for mass gatherings. By nipping organized protests in the bud, it has been trying to maintain social order while it attempts to find viable solutions for grievances. Its tactics, while often criticized by Western media, appear almost benign when compared to those of many police forces in other parts of the world like Brazil or even the United States, where violent police responses to mass protests like Black Lives Matter have captured headlines.

China's propaganda organs also should not be underestimated. With Xi Jinping's approval rating already high amongst the Chinese population, any additional affront to China by the United States will only solidify popular support for him and his administration, not unlike what happened to Putin's popularity at home after the US imposed sanctions following Russia's invasion of Crimea.

Another Cold War?

In the intricate web of geopolitics, there come times when diplomacy and negotiations break down. Tension and mistrust can reach a fever pitch in which actions that follow are often punitive. Past conflicts have often started with public denunciations followed by sanctions. What kind of effect will economic sanctions have on China if the United States enacts any?

To help answer this question we can look to history as the United States subjected China to economic sanctions once before, after the Communists took over in 1949. Yet even after the enormous setbacks of both Japanese attacks during World War II and the effects of a Civil War, these sanctions did not kill its economy. In fact, China slowly but surely began rebuilding economically, even after misguided leadership from Chairman Mao. The Chinese people endured severe tests of economic hardship, but the GDP still managed to grow steadily throughout Mao's reign. Only in four years out of his 27-year rule did China experience negative growth, and this was the result of extreme self-induced economic and political policies by Mao that were incredibly misinformed, not of anything the United States did to China. Of course, had the United States not imposed sanctions on China, China probably would have been far more advanced than it is today, but the sanctions themselves did not prevent its survival and growth.

If we look at more recent examples of other countries that have experienced sudden US sanctions, such as Russia, we also see a natural setback in their economies, but not a full-fledged economic collapse. After Russia's invasion of Crimea in 2014, US sanctions did cause negative GDP growth in subsequent quarters, but they also simultaneously hurt the countries that exported to Russia, namely Germany, Austria, and other Central European nations. The negative GDP growth, while tough on its citizens, actually galvanized the Russian people to become even more nationalistic and approving of their leader Vladimir Putin. Their economy, instead of falling apart, began adjusting to the new reality by developing new markets and strengthening political and economic relations with China, North Korea, Turkey, Iran, and others. If Russia, which has an economy that is less diverse and less robust than China's, was able to resist economic collapse with tough US sanctions, it then seems logical to extrapolate that China could also withstand economic sanctions without collapse being on the cards.

Ironically, when the Cold War ended and the Soviet Union transitioned to Russia and opened up to Western-style capitalism led by the United States, its economy and society collapsed. Why did this happen? A series of events that followed Gorbachev's resignation in 1991 put unsustainable pressure on the system. First, a large number of soldiers who were once deployed were sent home without jobs waiting for them, so there was a sudden surge of unemployment. Second, the United

States sent "economic advisors" to the former Soviet Union to help it transition from a Communist state to a capitalist one. The US policy position was that the Soviet Union needed to privatize its state-owned assets. The oligarchs who ran the various operations and facilities quickly bought these assets for a pittance since they had access to and knowledge about them that were denied to the average Russian. Once these insiders took possession of these state assets, they proceeded to renegotiate all the terms and conditions for operating them to suit their own profit interests. Almost overnight, the citizens of the former Soviet Union had experienced the shock of all their original social contracts being torn up. The prices for accessing basic needs like electricity and water soared in an instant. Pension funds and jobs that they had relied upon for the duration of their lives had suddenly disappeared. Turmoil and chaos ensued since people's livelihoods were turned upside down without warning.

China's leaders have studied this situation with a magnifying glass and have drawn lessons from the disintegration of the Soviet Union that they have sworn never to repeat. China's rotation of its central government personnel helps to deter corruption (people can't steal money today without a successor finding out in a couple of years by reading internal documents) and to make sure no one is so essential to an operation that he or she cannot be replaced. With such controls in place, the hijacking of state assets Soviet-style is less common and less harmful in China.

Worst Case Scenario?

If the world undergoes another world war, then all bets are off. Every economy would collapse. However, short of world war, China could still manage without complete collapse. As it advances, the ability for it to behave more like a developed world economy increases, because it would become more self-reliant and less vulnerable to external negative shocks.

China's impact on other economies around the globe would depend on the nature of the relationship between the countries and/or the region. For instance, countries that rely on commodity exports would certainly be impacted by a sharp slowdown in China. Commodity prices and volumes would fall, and unless there were another country that could substitute for China's import volume, those exporting countries would continue to hurt economically. First there would be layoffs, followed by second-order effects such as rating agency down-grades and widening credit spreads, which can also contribute to growing economic pain. Third-order effects would result from a combination of falling prices in financial markets actually weakening the exporting economy and its neighbors beyond the immediate commodity sectors.

However, for more developed countries, a sharp economic slowdown in China would have less of an impact simply because the world still primarily uses the US dollar for trade and financing transactions. Any seizing up of China's credit or banking system would not likely lead to a full-blown financial crisis like the one the world experienced in 2008, simply because the renminbi is still not as widely circulated and invested in outside of China's borders.

A possible worst case scenario may include China's capital account being liberalized too quickly in response to Wall Street pressures. If this happens, it could trigger a number of destabilizing effects such as large outflows from China's reserves, which could have a negative impact on its ability to meet working capital needs in trade obligations. Large outflows on a free-floating currency would also create significant volatility in the foreign exchange markets that could cause cross-border trade to come to a standstill. Consumption and outbound investment would also fall since a sharply lower renminbi would decrease the purchasing power of the Chinese in everything from bread to high-tech companies. With falling investment and rising producer prices from a sharply depreciated currency, China's GDP could head into negative territory in this scenario.

The government's response to these circumstances would likely be to hike interest rates to attract capital inflow as well as pump liquidity into the banking system to keep as many operations running as possible. While NPLs would rise as companies with foreign operations might find it impossible to stay solvent, the Chinese banks might also simply relax loan terms and make other adjustments in order to keep the companies from filing for bankruptcy.

The biggest risk would be financial contagion to other countries that do a lot of business with China. Since China has become the biggest market for many countries, including those in Europe and the Far East, those countries would be instantly exposed to any financial turmoil in China which would quickly translate into layoffs back home once manufacturing costs became unsustainable and profits fell. However, China's leadership most likely has considered this no-win scenario and probably will not lift its capital controls for the foreseeable future.

Even Black Swans Won't Kill

Events such as another world war, an asteroid, or a deadly disease outbreak that is the modern equivalent of the bubonic plague could certainly cause China's economy to collapse. But short of these extreme occurrences, one is hard-pressed to imagine a situation where the largest country in the world collapses when it is so well buttressed against coercion from outside economic forces with many policy options at its disposal while at the same time it is so widely integrated into the global economy. Rather than question whether China will collapse, one may as well ask: will humanity collapse? Or will capitalism itself collapse? From one perspective, China is simply a microcosm of humanity at large. China can't be easily analyzed in isolation because it is so intertwined with the world. To be fair, perhaps we should also entertain the opposite scenario: that China will save humanity.

4

Can China's Economy
Lift Us All?

Black swan or no black swan, China appears well fortified for the time being. In fact, it is so well buttressed that while many in the media want us to think of China as being the nation that could drag down the world economy, it may actually do the reverse. It is easy to see the numerous distortions that litter the landscape of China and conclude that the short-term prospects look dim. However, if one takes a longer-term perspective, China still has plenty of growth potential that can power it for generations, much the way the United States was able to become stronger after the Civil War and much stronger after World War II. As long as its leaders can implement the right policies at the right time, China could overcome its difficulties and even excel far beyond our current imaginations. Recall that it was China that saved the world from slumping into a global recession shortly after the 2008 global financial crisis by increasing its imports from the entire world to fuel its domestic infrastructure investment. No one quite expected an emerging economy to play the superhero in this global disaster. While a repeat of the same policies is unlikely to happen, China could reprise its role as savior if another economic crisis occurs in some other part of the world.

The United States has been regarded as the unbeatable superpower of the twenty-first century for good reason: its military is unparalleled; the US dollar is still the most dominant reserve currency in circulation by a mile; its economy is the largest in the world in nominal terms; and its media outreach is among the most influential and dominant on the global stage. Yet, despite all these undeniable strengths, the United States masks a number of vulnerabilities that could easily erupt into a full-scale crisis that would require China's help.

Chief among these vulnerabilities is the US economy, which has been lackluster ever since the 2008 crisis. While the official unemployment number has drifted to respectably low single digits, the actual number of people out of work has been growing far higher than this indicator would suggest. The labor force has shrunk to levels not seen in the last

30 years, which means that more people in the United States have been out of work for so long that they are not even counted in the unemployment numbers. Moreover, as reported by Alan Krueger, former Chairman of Obama's Council of Economic Advisers, the gains in employment in the United States for the years following the 2008 crisis have primarily been in part-time work, contractor work, or government services. Full-time work in the private sector has been going the way of the dinosaur, leaving more young people without a career and thus the financial means to start families.[21]

Other statistics point to the growing inequality and the growing lack of social mobility in the United States. As a result, its reputation as the land of opportunity for talented immigrants may become tarnished. European companies such as EV-Box from the Netherlands have discovered that even if their technology is proven in Europe, selling in the United States is a difficult exercise since obtaining certifications and other regulatory hoops have delayed their ability to be profitable for extended periods of time. Even home-grown entrepreneurs have found it difficult because the economy is riddled not only with anti-competitive regulations, but also with monopolies. While there are millions of people who try to start businesses, only hundreds receive funding from venture capital, which tends to concentrate in areas that happen to be in vogue at the time. Crowdfunding, which exploded after the JOBS (Jumpstart Our Business Startups) Act signed by President Obama in 2012, has since hit roadblocks. The regulators have significantly cut back on the number of licenses they issue for capital raising because they don't have the manpower to oversee the demand. Lack of job prospects can lead to population decline over time because economic discouragement prompts people to leave for greener pastures.

More worrisome about these trends is that when fewer and fewer people are participating in meaningful work, the potential for future innovation and dynamism also slows. When increasing numbers of companies replace workers with machines, the potential for insight and ground-breaking work that follows from insight can quickly diminish. This phenomenon would hold true regardless of whether the machine has replaced checkout counter assistants or Wall Street traders. The effect is the same. Even if the jobs being replaced may be seen as of low value and redundant, human insight that comes from noting patterns or deriving inspiration from making connections may be short-circuited when fewer people are taking part as full contributors to a society.

Since the United States prides itself as the leader in innovation and enjoys a giant lead over China in many high-tech areas, it is most vulnerable in losing this position. If US raw talent to fuel innovation were to dwindle, China could quickly bypass the United States in certain strategic areas such as the physical sciences, where there are more Chinese graduates than American graduates every year.

Another Achilles' heel is the US monetary system. Widely seen as wholly partial to Wall Street bankers as opposed to helping the economy, the Federal Reserve is suffering from severe credibility issues. Ever since Chairman Ben Bernanke engaged in massive quantitative easing to the tune of trillions of dollars to save the banks, the United States and the world economy have had subpar growth for one of the longest periods in history. The reason is that the money has flowed directly to large financial players so that they can speculate in financial markets, but it has not found a way to get into the pockets of everyday citizens. This broken transmission system is due to the fact that the Fed does not require the banks who borrow money from it to lend this out in the form of loans to the real economy. The borrowed money can simply be used for speculation in financial markets for a quick return. This has led to a world that is at the mercy of instability throughout the entire global financial system because speculative or "hot" money flows overwhelm the real economies that produce goods and services of real value. Everywhere in the world there is an abundance of capital, but a shortage of worthy investments. According to the Bank of International Settlements, in 2014 the total number of derivatives exceeded $700T, while the total GDP of the entire world economy according to the *CIA Factbook* was only $107T.

This kind of monetary order creates a number of perverse incentives and political outcomes. Chief among them is the fact that it undermines the very democratic fabric that made America great. When the founders first debated whether to have a central bank, many of the objections had to do with the fact that those who have the license to control money would have an inordinate amount of power and create the conditions for abuse by a privileged few over the many, the very conditions they sought to escape in the first place by leaving the Old Continent. Alexander Hamilton, who proposed America's first central bank in the 1780s, made very clear that the institution he envisioned would strictly release funds for the sole purpose of nation building. The central bank, in other words, would not engage in the sort of activities that the Federal

Reserve has been engaging in and would not support or enable the speculative behavior of private banks today.

Oddly enough, the kind of monetary system that Hamilton advocated and that was approved of by the founding fathers is the kind of system being practiced by China. The Chinese have used the Central Bank and the state-owned banks primarily to support nation building by extending loans mostly to infrastructure projects both inside and outside the country. This happened in a big way following the 2008 financial crisis, but that policy was in place both before and after that period to ensure steady growth in the real economy. The Chinese banks do not engage in proprietary trading for their own account in financial markets and do not service the largest institutional money management firms the same way Goldman Sachs can with firms like BlackRock and Blackstone. As a result, their money is more correlated to the rapid advancement and progress of Chinese society. By making its real economy robust through government-led investments in its own soft and hard infrastructure, China has built a solid foundation from which stronger growth and innovation can be self-sustaining. In contrast, the US monetary system has stifled the fortunes of many while the large financial institutions continued to reap extraordinary benefits that accrue only to themselves and have little multiplier effect. With zero interest rates, most people are losing money to inflation if they keep their savings in a bank, and because capital is not democratized, they have little access to it to get their dreams off the ground.

So unlike the previous collapses in history, where empires fell apart because they eventually ran out of money that was based on precious metals, today's collapse would be the inability to sustain real wealth creation through productivity. Money is no longer the gating factor since all money now is fiat money which can be created out of thin air by the banks or central banks. In fact, central banks around the world have purposely engaged in shoring up credibility of fiat money by purchasing stocks and bonds of all nations, but particularly those of the United States, to keep them elevated in financial markets. At the same time, they are actively shorting commodities, particularly precious metals like gold, in order to discredit the investors who have cried foul against the runaway money printing of the current financial system. By keeping this system in place, they know that they won't lose their power because they can always control man-made money. As long as the massive money printing doesn't create unwanted runaway inflation, they think they are safe. They have accomplished low inflation by keeping the money circulation limited to the privileged few elites who have experienced extraordinary increases in wealth while the rest of their world's populations have only received the crumbs from the table in today's actual practice of "trickle-down economics," which was first popularized during the Reagan era. The financial elites who have access to the fiat money first hand accumulate it for themselves and distribute it through their business dealings with the other elite organs in society, like the mainstream media and defense contractors, who have the same interest in protecting the status quo. This tight-knit circle of elites makes it incredibly difficult for anyone on the outside to break into the club and create competition for the status quo because access to capital is so difficult. With most of the capital out of reach of the average person, inflation remains low and productivity remains below potential while capital markets stay elevated to enrich the privileged few. But one weakness is that without a broad talent base to cultivate, the innovators from the outer fringes could abandon this rigged network.

Of course, the United States can mirror the Saudi Arabian model or the Indian model, in which the privileged few can rule seemingly indefinitely while the masses remain poor and dependent on a welfare state. This scenario has a chance of working out if the "slow boil of a frog," to borrow an analogy from Al Gore's *An Inconvenient Truth*, keeps the masses ignorant and sufficiently powerless to fight back. But even if this ruling class cannot be removed from power, their days are numbered when there isn't sufficient talent and brain power to come up with solutions to global problems. Today we have melting glaciers and potentially devastating diseases like the Ebola virus. Perhaps tomorrow there will be even more serious threats from nature that are completely unforeseen. Such problems cannot be solved if the ruling elites do not broaden the talent base by sharing the wealth and opportunities with all levels of society. These problems can quickly overwhelm any system that is only prepared for military combat and financial manipulation and woefully underfunded in other areas. Given this dark scenario, a more broadly based wealth creation system that China has implemented will stand a much greater chance of combatting such threats in the future than the United States will if it does not reform itself to actually be the land of opportunity again instead of just paying the idea lip service.

Thus, in the short and medium term, China does

have a number of favorable things going for it that will keep it from collapsing. The ability to grow its middle class will be relatively low-hanging fruit. Its embryonic capital markets offer room for growth before it catches up to US levels. The expansion into other countries, especially into developing countries that still have expanding populations and a shortage of needs being met, represents an enormous opportunity. And finally, the expansion of the RMB can create trillions of dollars worth of wealth without creating runaway inflation, as long as the money is put to productive use.

In the long term, China's growth will slow and mirror the growth rate of the rest of the world simply because it is limited by its boundaries. Its growth will be determined by its own rate of innovation. The more successful it is in keeping the drivers of innovation in place in its economy, such as keeping overregulation from stifling progress and keeping tax rates low so that incentive remains for entrepreneurs, the more likely China's economy will remain robust for decades to come.

Far from the pessimists' view that China's economy will collapse, one must remember to question the assumptions behind such a view: whether they are about China's lack of the kind of reform that conforms to Western predetermined but erroneous notions or simply reflect a lack of understanding of how modern monetary systems work. And while a number of mainstream economists argue that countries can't expect rapid growth to last more than a decade because they all revert to the mean, China has defied theory by growing on average 10% a year over the last two decades. Obviously that growth rate can't last forever, not because China lacks productive capacity, but because of the inadequate consumption demand in the current environment. But if China can overcome this challenge by expanding its higher education and increasing the wealth of other developing economies with the same recipe it used to grow its own economy, then the lack of consumption demand in the world economy can easily become a thing of the past. Can the entirety of Africa, Latin America, Southeast Asia, and Central Asia eventually be made to become as productive as China? Who knows? Only time will tell. But in the meantime, China is too busy making things happen in the world that many economic conferences would think are impossible.

Epilogue

This book has suggested many additional themes and departure points, not the least of which is that, in the very long term, capitalism in its current incarnation, East or West, will face a crisis. The rise of populism in the age of President Trump already is an early indicator that societies cannot remain cohesive when populations grow faster than the well-paying jobs available. As more and more workers are displaced by technology and become marginalized, either society will grow discontented from boredom with a benevolent government or more people will become dispossessed and starve under an illiberal government, thus planting the seeds for terrorism and revolution. Moreover, workers' endeavor and productivity need to be tied to reward. When capitalism is driven only by pure profits, it leads to extremes in wealth gaps as well as corruption in the system that undercuts outcomes for everybody. Such wealth gaps can be created, for instance, when hedge funds and banks are allowed to engage in speculation and other rent-seeking behavior which enables individuals managing those entities to usurp the rewards of productive activity. Taken to extremes, such a scenario will eventually kill the incentive for individual effort. But since people inherently need to find meaning in life, work and exploration must exist to provide such meaning for humanity to continue to thrive and evolve. We need to find a more sustainable model in which each person is valued for what he or she can contribute and the diversity of the world's resources is valued more than the acquisition of money.

Notes

1. A. Lee, *What the US Can Learn from China: An Open-Minded Guide to Treating Our Greatest Competitor as Our Greatest Teacher* (San Francisco: Berrett–Koehler Publishers, 2012).
2. M. Zhang, "China's 'mountain' of foreign debt is not as scary as it looks," *International Business Times*, February 18, 2014 (available at: http://www.ibtimes.com/chinas-mountain-foreign-debt-not-scary-it-looks-1556107).
3. H. Yuanyuan and Z. Hao, "China's non-performing loans on the rise," *China Daily*, updated July 22, 2015 (available at: http://www.chinadaily.com.cn/business/2015-07/22/content_21379181.htm).
4. Agence France-Presse, "China's debt is 250% of GDP and 'could be fatal', says government expert," *Guardian*, June 16, 2016 (available at: https://www.theguardian.com/business/2016/jun/16/chinas-debt-is-250-of-gdp-and-could-be-fatal-says-government-expert).

5. J. Edwards, "How China accumulated $28 trillion in debt in such a short time," *Business Insider*, January 6, 2016 (available at: http://www.businessinsider.com/china-debt-to-gdp-statistics-2016-1).

6. N. Somasundaram and B. Purvis, "The mother of peak debt – Japan's total debt-to-GDP ratio stands at 600%," *Bloomberg Business*, August 31, 2016 (available at: http://www.brotherjohnf.com/mother-peak-debt-japans-total-debt-gdp-ratio-stands-600/).

7. M. Pomerleano, "Corporate financial restructuring in Asia: implications for financial stability," *BIS Quarterly Review*, September 2007, p. 84 (JEL classification: G32, G38) (available at: http://www.bis.org/publ/qtrpdf/r_qt0709.pdf).

8. N. Zhang and T. Wang, *Here Comes More Credit* (UBS Research, 2016).

9. R. Rutkowski, "Will China finally tackle overcapacity?" (Petersen Institute for International Economics China Economic Watch, April 22, 2014) (available at: https://piie.com/blogs/china-economic-watch/will-china-finally-tackle-overcapacity).

10. *CIA World Factbook 2016*.

11. J. Lin, *Demystifying the Chinese Economy* (New York: Cambridge University Press, 2012), p. 98.

12. H. Xie and G. Wildau, "China makes fresh bid to curb shadow banking, contain debt risk," *Reuters*, January 6, 2014 (available at: http://www.reuters.com/article/us-china-economy-shadow-banking-idUSBREA0503T20140106).

13. Y. Deng, "Understanding the risks of China's local government debts and its linkage with property

markets" (International Symposium on Housing and International Stability in China, Chinese University of Hong Kong, Shenzhen, 2015; available at: https://www.imf.org/external/np/seminars/eng/2015/HousingChina/pdf/Session%203_YDeng.pdf).

14. V. Lin, "China's shadow banking system now 78 pc and growing, says Moodys," *South China Morning Post*, July 27, 2016 (available at: http://www.scmp.com/business/money/money-news/article/1995453/chinas-shadow-banking-system-now-78pc-gdp-and-growing-says).

15. Financial Stability Board, *Global Shadow Banking Monitoring Report 2015*.

16. Credit Suisse Equity Research, *Analysing Chinese Grey Income*, August 6, 2010 (available at: https://doc.research-and-analytics.csfb.com/docView?language=ENG&source=ulg&format=PDF&document_id=857531571&serialid=WabTv3n9BdHCgZ3T53I97qLKOv%2BqNcskKT70z4WvVpI%3D).

17. T. Wang, *UBS RMB Chartbook* (UBS Investment Research, 2016).

18. P. Spence, "China's yuan becomes world's fifth most used payment currency," *The Telegraph*, January 28, 2015 (available at: http://www.telegraph.co.uk/finance/currency/11373715/Chinas-yuan-becomes-worlds-fifth-most-used-payment-currency.html).

19. R. Aitken, "Chinese RMB consolidates second most used currency ranking for DC trade transactions," *Forbes*, February 28, 2015 (available at: http://www.forbes.com/sites/rogeraitken/2015/02/28/chinese-rmb-consolidates-second-most-used-curr

ency-ranking-for-dc-trade-transactions/#162a2b72 d8cb).

20. Ludovica Iaccino, "China: more than 82 million live below poverty line," *International Business Times*, October 16, 2014 (available at: http://www.ibtimes. co.uk/china-more-82-million-people-live-below-pov erty-line-1470313).

21. Rebecca Ungarino, "Burdened with record amount of debt, graduates delay marriage," NBC News, October 7, 2014 (available at: http://www.nbcnews. com/business/personal-finance/burdened-record-amount-debt-graduates-delay-marriage-n219371).